PRAISE FOR BANINE

'I started to leaf through the book and was soon engrossed... So vividly and wittily does the author reveal to us an utterly unfamiliar world'
TEFFI, AUTHOR OF MEMORIES: FROM MOSCOW TO THE BLACK SEA

'A delightful memoir of an eventful life set against the helter-skelter of the 20th century... Banine herself shines through as an intelligent and independent spirit, longing for her own self-determination'
FINANCIAL TIMES

'Every so often a voice emerges from the archive so vivid that it seems impossible that it should ever have been forgotten...'
EVENING STANDARD

BANINE (1905–1992) was born Umm El-Banu Assadullayeva, into a wealthy family in Baku, then part of the Russian Empire. Following the Russian Revolution and the subsequent fall of the Azerbaijan Democratic Republic, Banine was forced to flee her home country—first to Istanbul, and then to Paris. In Paris she formed a wide circle of literary acquaintances including Nicos Kazantzakis, André Malraux, Ivan Bunin and Teffi and eventually began writing herself. *Parisian Days* continues the story that began with *Days in the Caucasus*, which is also available from Pushkin Press.

ANNE THOMPSON-AHMADOVA is a writer and translator from Azerbaijani, French and Russian. She lived in Baku for twenty years, moving there in 1997 initially to set up a Caucasus bureau for the BBC Monitoring Service.

PARISIAN DAYS

BANINE

TRANSLATED FROM THE FRENCH
BY ANNE THOMPSON-AHMADOVA

PUSHKIN PRESS CLASSICS

Pushkin Press
Somerset House, Strand
London WC2R 1LA

Parisian Days was first published as *Jours parisiens* in Paris, 1947

First published by Pushkin Press in 2023
This edition published 2024

1 3 5 7 9 8 6 4 2

ISBN 13: 978 1 78227 803 0

Designed and typeset by Tetragon, London
Printed and bound in the United Kingdom by Clays Ltd, Elcograf S.p.A.

www.pushkinpress.com

Contents

Foreword by the Translator

At the opening of *Parisian Days*, a young passenger waits in trepidation for the Orient Express to pull into the Gare de Lyon. Author Banine is on the threshold of a new life, far from her native Azerbaijan. She writes of her introduction to Paris in the Roaring Twenties, her evolution from 'Caucasian goose' into shy fashion model, allowing occasional glimpses of her childhood to give background to the story.

Banine was born in 1905 in the booming oil city of Baku, then part of the Russian Empire. Ummulbanu Asadullayeva, to use her full name, was the granddaughter of peasants who had become fabulously wealthy through oil. In her first memoir, *Days in the Caucasus*, she described her upbringing by a Baltic German governess and a devoutly Muslim grandmother who swore like a trooper. Banine's life of long summers in the country house and winters of lessons and avid reading was upended in 1920 when Russian Bolshevik troops entered Baku.

In Paris, Banine finds herself amongst émigrés from all corners of the former empire who fled the Revolution and Civil War. Some, including authors Bunin and Teffi, become her friends. Banine resists Teffi's calls to write in Russian, though she speaks it fluently, and prefers to write in French, the language of her beloved city. As she makes clear in *Parisian Days*, Banine feels Azerbaijani and Caucasian, not Russian.

Banine uses real names for some members of her family, and pseudonyms for others. In *Parisian Days* she changes her sister Surayya's name to Maryam, and calls Surayya's husband Shamsi, rather than Murad, probably to protect their privacy. In both memoirs Banine uses the name Zuleykha for her sister Kubra. I mention it here as Kubra Asadullayeva enjoyed success as a Cubist painter in France. Most of her work, including portraits of Banine, is thought to be in private collections.

Banine's first published work was a novel *Nami*, which came out in Paris in 1942. *Nami* is set in Baku and Russia during the revolution and Civil War and its eponymous heroine is reminiscent of both Banine and her stepmother Amina. Three years later, Banine's memoir *Days in the Caucasus* established her in Parisian literary circles. *Parisian Days* is the sequel, published by René Julliard in 1947. Banine substantially reworked *Parisian Days* before republishing it with Gris Banal in 1990. It is this revised version that has been translated here.

The most successful of Banine's later works was an account of her conversion to Roman Catholicism, *I Chose Opium*. This too had a sequel, *Afterwards*, to respond to readers who wanted to know what happened next. Banine translated widely into French, including work by Dostoevsky, Tatyana Tolstaya and the German author Ernst Jünger who became a good friend.

Banine died in Paris in 1992 at the age of eighty-six.

As her father, and even more so her grandfathers, are famous figures in the history of Azerbaijan, the Soviet authorities invited Banine to visit Baku, an invitation she did not take up. 'I would be lying if I said that I do not regret it now,' Banine wrote in

1985 in an author's note accompanying a reissue of *Days in the Caucasus*. She herself came to public attention in Azerbaijan only in the late 1980s, when the Soviet newspaper *Literaturnaya gazeta* published an article about her friendship and correspondence with Bunin.

Banine's work was not published in Azerbaijani until 1992, when Hamlet Qoca's translation of *Days in the Caucasus* came out in an abridged version (in which some of the references to sex were omitted).

Wherever Banine used an Azerbaijani, German or Russian expression in *Parisian Days*, I have preserved those words and added an English version where needed. The footnotes are Banine's unless otherwise indicated.

The language of Azerbaijan is known as Azerbaijani, Azeri or Azerbaijani Turkish. Banine used the version *Azéri*, so in the translation I opted for the closest equivalent in English, Azeri.

ANNE THOMPSON-AHMADOVA

Arrival in the Promised Land

The Orient Express charges at full throttle towards the Promised Land. The racket is deafening as it is hurled from track to track in a wild dance. Its language of steel speaks to me of freedom and joy while it sweeps me towards the realm of my fantasies, towards the dazzling moment of reunion I longed for during four years of revolution, ruin and terror amid the rubble of an abolished world.

Four years of separation from my closest relatives, who left the Caucasus when it was still free while I remained alone with my father, a minister of the ephemeral independent Republic of Azerbaijan. When the Russians recaptured the Caucasus, he was thrown in prison for the crime of being rich, and at fifteen years of age I was thrown into the prison of a forced marriage. During those deathly years, in the depths of my despair, I took refuge in dreams, constructing entire worlds, imagining the craziest things—incredible happiness, conquests and victories.

At last I am actually experiencing these unique moments in reality, as they usher me into the dawn of a paradise. Rigid from head to toe in almost unbearable anticipation, throat dry, chest heavy, my seventeen-year-old heart beating like a demented clock, I watch the march of life through the window. Emotion blinds me to the ugly suburbs passing before my eyes, instead I see dreams, my refuge during those years of cold, of near-starvation, of fear. I would soon achieve conquests and victories and never let them go. One tremendous victory was already mine: attaining the Promised Land. I was almost there, after fleeing first the Caucasus, then Constantinople, where I abandoned my husband in a flurry of false promises. He hoped to join me, while I hoped never to see him again; poor man, like me a victim of History, which crushes us in its path.

*

The canopy of the Gare de Lyon closes over the train, covering it with its shadow. It goes slower and slower until it stops at last, and my heart stops with it; I am about to die. But no; expiring, gasping, trembling, I manage to step down onto the platform without dropping dead, and at last I see them through my tears. There are four of them: my beautiful stepmother Amina, my childhood love; my two sisters Zuleykha and Maryam; and finally my arrogant, unbearable brother-in-law.* I find myself wrapped around each neck in turn and I cry and laugh and feel a happiness that even death could not snatch from me. But I do

---

* In *Parisian Days* and *Days in the Caucasus*, Banine uses real names for some members of her family, and pseudonyms for others. For reasons that she does not explain, she calls her sister Kubra 'Zuleykha' in both memoirs, while she uses the real names of her sister Surayya and brother-in-law Murad in *Days in the Caucasus*, but calls them 'Maryam' and 'Shamsi' respectively in *Parisian Days*. [Translator's note.]

not die, my tears dry, everyone talks and laughs at once, they ask me questions, I answer any old how. Sentimentality overcomes me for a moment, but is checked: my family takes a dim view of mawkishness, inclined as they are towards irony, sometimes brutally so. And my brilliant brother-in-law Shamsi is here, who has a cruel wit; he won't let us fall into a vat of rose water. He holds a stick and taps it drily, studying me with a mocking gaze that does not bode well: he finds my *charchaf*—a half-veil worn by Turkish women—my off-the-peg suit from a shop in Constantinople and my air of a provincial goose hilarious. His stick points at my hips, which are luxuriant, and I feel myself accused of a crime. He bursts out:

'No, really, this is a costume for a show which will be called "Progress and the Odalisque"; a *charchaf* in Paris, the eyebrows of a Caucasian carter, and that suit! It's perfect for Tashkent. And that derrière is perfect for Abdul Hamid's harem! We'll have to hire a wheelbarrow to carry it.'

Amina and my sisters angrily tell him to leave me alone, but this sets him off all the more.

I don't want to lose face so I laugh, but I don't have to try too hard: life is sweet, I am living a fairy tale that cannot be marred by a few discordant details. I am stunned by the bustle of the station, the noise, the movement—and by the emotion that the present happiness, in contrast with the four years of suffering, is wringing from my sensibility. I feel as though I have escaped from an icy cave, full of shadows, and climbed up towards a sunlit meadow.

Already a novelist without knowing it, I notice, despite this inner turmoil, my sisters' extraordinary make-up. That Zuleykha, the painter, should be outrageous is not such a surprise: she is committed to colour, to the artist's boldness, the creative person's extravagance. But I am astounded that modest, shy Maryam should sport dusky eyelids, lashes laden with mascara like branches of a fir tree laden with snow, cheeks reminiscent of geraniums in their first bloom, a thick layer of powder and lips the colour of oxblood. I notice and file away, but say nothing, of course.

Zuleykha's garb also attains the heights of artistic expression: strange objects hang everywhere; a flowerpot-shaped hat is pushed over her eyes; huge earrings brush her neck which is adorned with an exotic necklace. A belt with Aztec designs is placed, not around her waist, but on her hips in accordance with the current laws of fashion. Beneath this fantastical clothing, I find my sister voluble, exuberant, full of life and verve.

We get into a spacious red taxi of a kind no longer with us, alas, which one could get into without bending double and proceeding to collapse onto the back seat like a sack of potatoes. My single suitcase sits next to the driver. The great adventure begins. I AM IN PARIS.

Paris… To grasp the full significance of I AM IN PARIS, one must have believed oneself locked up for ever in a detested city, lost at the edge of the world; one has to have dreamt of Paris for long, dragging years, as I dreamt of it in the heart of my native city, where, paradoxical though it may seem, I truly lived in exile.

For a soul fascinated by this name, Paris is the beacon illuminating paradise; the dream become stone and streets, squares and statues, erected throughout a long and turbulent history. It is the splendour of all fantasies, a world where micro-worlds clash or meld, creating an extraordinary wealth of life.

Deeply unfaithful by nature, I have remained faithful to Paris, despite a half-century of intimacy, of familiarity with the attractions and aversions, as in all intimacy—above all, the aversions of habit and monotony.

Dreamers of the whole world, I address you in particular, you who know the virtue and the poison of dreams. Their virtue: they are our opium in the grey monotony of the everyday, our shelter from laws and kings; our granite in the quicksand of the world; our daily brioche when we lack even bread. Their poison: if by a miracle our dreams come true, we feel the cursed 'is that it?' Life in its impurity tarnishes their perfection, which exists only in the imagination, and disappointment poisons us; 'Is that it?'

Now, during the first days of my life in Paris, this *was* it. Everything was beautiful, young, interesting, amusing, full of promise. Even on arrival, I was enchanted by the ugly, sooty surroundings of the Gare de Lyon, as this was where I took my first steps as a Parisienne. Then it was the marvellous design of the Rue de Rivoli; the even more perfect design of the Place de la Concorde, which brings to mind a rock garden; and the Champs-Élysées, where the driver took us at our request. We drove down the prestigious avenue, which in those days, half a century ago, radiated elegance with nothing to spoil it. There was just one shop—Guerlain—two or three cafes—Le Select, Le Fouquet—two fashion houses and the Hotel Claridge. Though democratization has its virtues, it had yet to disfigure the elegant, snobbish avenue. No loose sweets were on sale, no discount dresses, no plastic shoes, no handmade rugs or bags of peanuts. Cinemas did not entice you every ten paces with their posters and pornographic offerings for all ages, sexes and preferences.

We drove slowly up the Champs-Élysées to the Arc de Triomphe, which had its greatest triumph over me; we descended the Avenue du Bois, or had it already been rechristened Avenue Foch? Without leaving the finer districts we reached La Muette and Rue Louis Boilly, where my parents rented an apartment on the ground floor of a handsome building. We were to stay in these largely residential areas until we had run out of jewellery brought from over there, the sole, slim remains of our oil barons' fortune, democratized, collectivized, nationalized, volatilized in the revolutionary explosion, which consumed all our privileges in its flames.

As we drove down Avenue du Bois, I recalled for a few moments another 'boulevard', the one running along the Caspian where I had strolled for so many years beneath the shade of a few stunted trees, my soul in distress, my spirit elsewhere—in Paris, to be exact. It was thanks to that explosion that I was here at last, and I much preferred to be poor here than rich over there. No, it's not a case of 'the grass is always greener'. When just a child, as I have written elsewhere, I mentally ruined my paternal and maternal families to gain the right to marry Ruslan, the handsome gardener with the air of a prince from *The Thousand and One Nights*. He was one of the twelve near-slaves whose job was to water an estate in the desert. As for our ruination, my wishes had been fully granted. Sadly, it was not the seductive Ruslan's arms that welcomed me on my wedding night; this good fortune had been granted to Jamil, whom I abhorred.

I could not complain, as the decrees of fate had replaced Ruslan with emigration, where I was certain I would meet Ruslans a thousand times more handsome, a thousand times more seductive and from a slightly more polished social class (after all). Steeped in *The Thousand and One Nights*, I imagined the future as one of Ali Baba's caves, where I would find fabulous treasure. Only one of all these treasures never occurred to my otherwise fertile imagination: that I would one day become a French writer and be able to write these lines.

*

My father was waiting for us in the entrance. He must have been watching for the taxi.

It was three years to the day, in Batumi, that I had watched him on the deck of a Compagnie Paquet ship as it moved out into the Black Sea towards Constantinople, towards Paris. He was leaving, but I was staying behind, and, worse, staying with my husband, who would take me back to Baku to continue our ridiculous conjugal life. How I suffered. We speak of a 'broken heart' and we are right; mine was shattered. Not from seeing my father leave, but from seeing him leave without me. Like Prometheus, I remained bound to an imaginary rock in the Caucasus and no Heracles would save me from my not-so-beloved.

Freedom, comfortable living conditions and, doubtless, the absence of fear had rejuvenated my father. He looked relaxed, was well dressed, and stood tall. I remembered so well his hunched back, his weary air, his prison clothes that by themselves can demean a man, and his poor smile when he saw me through the bars clutching the cooking pot into which my aunt, his sister, had poured the stew made specially for him. I lugged the heavy pot to the distant prison in the cold or fierce heat, but it brought him some comfort in his wretched detention.

That situation, with more than a whiff of melodrama, seemed unreal here. In this elegant apartment, where all was comfort and peace, the prison in the black suburb of Baku —black because it is situated in an oil zone—seemed like a nightmare. And in reality, what else was it?

We embraced with what might pass as tenderness between a reticent father and a daughter intimidated by him. The strangely expressive gaze of his black, shining eyes robbed me of any desire to be effusive. Had he ever treated me warmly? Never, I thought, not even when I visited him in prison. There was always a wall between us with no abandon on either side. He had never been really hard towards me, but I was afraid of him nonetheless, and this fear had prevented me from following the man I thought I loved and made me accept another, whom I definitely hated, solely because my father had expressed his wish for this to happen.

It is hard to grasp what the figure of the father once meant in the Islamic world from which we had come. Invested with an authority second only to that of God, he would treat his children like subjects without rights and was free to impose anything on them except death. It is quite possible that in primitive tribes ruled by Islamic law he was accorded this right too.

My father had a remarkable trait that was to become more pronounced with age—liberalism. Was it dictated by intelligence, indifference, or secret inclinations that we can hardly control, are hardly aware of? Nonetheless, this liberalism had allowed us, his daughters, to be brought up in the Western style at a time when this was still frowned upon in Islam. His second wife, my stepmother Amina, was also a beneficiary, but sometimes abused it. And soon he was to give us further proof of his broad-mindedness.

I was infinitely grateful to him for bringing me to Paris alone; perhaps to allow me to divorce later, and to put an end to a marriage he had so cruelly forced upon me? How I hoped that this was so. The idea of meeting this husband again, who displeased me in every respect, cast an occasional pall over my happiness at returning to my status as a young girl, at beginning my life again at the point I had lost it four years ago, but this time in an entirely new world, in this legendary Paris for which my soul had longed 'as a hart longs for flowing streams'.

I accepted the drawbacks in advance: I would give in to Zuleykha's customary bullying, her 'you'll know when you're my age', pronounced in a superior tone; I would listen submissively to her advice and that of Amina; I would carry out their orders with military discipline; in short, I was ready to do anything to leave my husband. If necessary, I would even go to bed before the others, as I had during my childhood; Fräulein Anna's '*Kinder, schlafen gehen!*' still rang in my ears like a sentence to the galleys. All of this was better than Jamil.

After embracing my father I turned, following an unspoken hierarchy, towards a boy of eight, my half-brother. Having forgotten me during the past four years, he stared at me in astonishment without the least sign of pleasure. Light skin, brown eyes, chestnut hair—with the look of a blonde Aryan he had inherited from his North Caucasian mother, he was out of place among our tribe doomed to black agate and other signs of oriental ancestry. We were Aryan too, and very pure at that, as Persian blood ran in our veins—but we were brown Aryans.

Another rung down in the hierarchy brought me face to face with my brother's tutor, a short old man, well groomed, with round, bewildered chicken eyes, who walked carefully on legs so bowed that they met only at the feet.

Further down the social scale were the cook and the maid who, as expressive French women, gave cries of joy and amazement when they saw me.

'Oh, mademoiselle is a madame? She's so young!'

'Mademoi— madame has such beautiful eyes.'

A stock compliment for want of anything better.

Yes, in those days, the race of Frenchwomen who went into domestic service was not yet extinct. Such service is judged humiliating today, and who would deny that it is thankless work? But is it so much better to type all day for a boss who is often difficult, or to work in a factory? It would appear so, to judge from the evidence. But in those legendary days when Social Security had yet to be set up, there were authentic French 'bonnes'.

I realize that I shall often have to refer to 'those days' as if to a different, bygone era. And with good reason: the changes that have come about in this half-century are so enormous that the world really is transformed. There is no point in enumerating these changes, as there are so many. I'll note one detail in passing, though: the end of the Rue Louis-Boilly, which today leads to the Boulevard Périphérique, in 'those days' overlooked the city fortifications where we were well advised not to venture at night—its inhabitants were rumoured to have a penchant for the most sinister crimes. Nor was it a pleasant stroll to cross the Parc de la Muette once darkness fell, lecherous men popping up like weeds behind every bush. The fear they inspired in us bordered on hysteria. So we lived between two danger zones: the *'fortifs'* and the lechers' park.

*

My Parisian apprenticeship began the very afternoon of my arrival in the privacy of the bedroom that I was to share with Zuleykha. It was just the three of us: Maryam, Zuleykha and me. When Zuleykha marched in she went straight to her nightstand and took out a cigarette holder the length of her forearm. Placing a cigarette in it with aplomb, she lit it and blew out a regal cloud of smoke that hit me in the face, causing a coughing fit. Then she proudly declared: 'I'm getting married.'

'Oh!' I cried, with curiosity and delight.

I considered it good news on two counts: first, because any marriage is inherently an auspicious event and the disaster of mine was merely an accident of the October Revolution—the revolution, always the revolution. Second, at the age of seventeen I found it awkward to have been married for two years while Zuleykha, four years my senior, was still an old maid. It was humiliating, unnatural. This reversal of roles was a breach of Islamic custom, perhaps even of a more widely accepted tradition. So I was very pleased to know that my sister was back on track.

'Who is he? A Caucasian?'

Paris was teeming with émigrés from every corner of the Russian Empire and our corner, the Caucasus, was well represented.

'Certainly not, I've had enough of Caucasians! He's Spanish. Catholic, of course.'

This took my breath away. I didn't know what to say, given the enormity of her choice, which according to our best traditions would lead her straight to hell. Finally, I dared to venture, 'And Papa?'

'What about Papa? He won't eat me! Anyway, I'm of age now. And we're not in Baku any longer, Islam is a long way away, everything is a long way away, everything has changed. Papa? Well, I'm going to talk to him about my José soon.'

I thought I detected a healthy dose of bravado in her confidence, but I also knew she was capable of great bravery, and admired her unreservedly for it, I who was so timorous.

'I'd never dare,' said Maryam, who was timorous too.

I supported her with alacrity, 'Nor would I.'

I knew what I was saying: hadn't I missed a perhaps model destiny because of this lack of courage, which weighed me down like a yoke? A yoke that prevented me from saying a liberating 'no' to my father when he asked me to marry Jamil; that stopped me from leaving with Andrey Massarin, a Christian too, but worse, much worse, a revolutionary and a Bolshevik! I could have run away with him but, paralysed by fear, I gave him up to marry someone else. Fear is my worst enemy, and may have ruined my life. How I hated it, and hate it still.

Sometimes, on the path of life where we grope our way forwards or, alternatively, forge ahead without giving it much thought, we see a treacherous fork appear before us, forcing us to make a choice on which our whole future depends. Left or right? How can we know where happiness lies, where misfortune lurks? Our sole consolation will be to think that our choice was illusory, as it had been predetermined since time immemorial.

Zuleykha found herself before a fork in the road that did not trouble her in the least, because her choice appeared so compelling to her. She knew what she wanted.

'A Christian,' I said, 'a Christian. He knows nothing of Islam. He may hate it. We have always fought, them and us.'

'Well, we've been wrong,' Zuleykha replied with authority, vigorously flicking the ash from her cigarette.

And the ash fell on the millions of Muslim and Christian warriors who had fought from the Hegira onwards; on the crusaders of the eight Crusades, the last of which ended with the death of St Louis at Carthage; on José's compatriots, led by the very Catholic Ferdinand and Isabella, who drove the Moors out of Spain; on the armies of John of Austria, who destroyed the Turks at Lepanto; on the troops of John Sobieski, king of Poland, and those same Turks laying siege to Vienna—and on others, on many others. Zuleykha's ash buried them all beneath the same opprobrium and her love for José transformed all these confrontations into idiotic children's games; and how could one say with certainty that they had not been idiots?

'And if you are making a mistake in marrying him?' Maryam asked.

'I never make mistakes. And you should know, my poor retards, that I have been his mistress for the past six months.'

This astounding news silenced the two retards. We gazed at Zuleykha, eyes round in incredulity, as obligatory virginity on the day of a wedding—for the girl, needless to say—was a dogma one could not even contemplate disobeying, as solid as the Kaaba in Mecca.

'You're mad,' I cried, this time in a fit of righteous indignation. 'Before marriage!'

Even my cousin Gulnar, so liberally shameless, had kept her virginity for her wedding night. What better authority on dissolute morals could I invoke?

'My dear,' Zuleykha replied, belching out smoke like a steam train moving off. Large puffs billowed from her nose and mouth at once.

'My dear, let me repeat—we are in Paris, thanks be to the October Revolution, and all that twaddle has been consigned to the dustbin once and for all.' After a slight pause she condescended, 'I'll take you to his studio soon. You should know that he's a painter, an accomplished artist. Another reason why madame' (a nod in Maryam's direction) 'has never deigned to meet him.'

'You know very well… Shamsi…'

Maryam tucked her head between her shoulders. Condemned by nature to self-effacement, she submitted without demur to the dominance of those around her and of circumstance, letting herself be bullied by one and all. Her current position between a tyrannical husband and an imperious sister was torture for her.

'Yes, Shamsi the Magnificent—what percentage of noble blood does his lineage have?—is shocked at the idea of being related to a Christian, to a painter without fame or fortune—for now.'

She raised her shoulders furiously, and her earrings jingled merrily like little bells.

'Keep turning your nose up at José, I couldn't give a damn and I'm marrying him anyway. Look at her, this fine flower of the Azerbaijani aristocracy who dares to look down on an artist. Let me remind you that our grandfather ate the stones on his land, and that was the size of a pocket handkerchief. It was not because of anything he'd done that he saw oil gushing from those stones. And let me remind you too that we've had all that oil taken away from us, down to the last drop, and we'll never get it back, for all the cherished illusions of these moronic émigrés. All we have left are memories and a host of pretensions. Oh, we've got sacks full of them, pretensions, we former petroleum princes.'

She was off on a passionate diatribe, full of gall and vitriol, against snobbery, aristocrats true and false, plutocrats in general and Muslims of the whole world. She pilloried wealth, the idleness of those who possess it, superstitions, religions that tear one another apart in the name of a good and merciful God. She certainly loved her José, who inspired her to such fiery oratory. As for me, steeped in four years of revolutionary propaganda, my ears still ringing with slogans such as 'religion is the opium of the people', 'man's exploitation of man' and other truths and half-truths, I was beginning to come round to her point of view.

But since I had neither her courage nor her strength, I could not see myself standing up to my father. But during his imprisonment, as though liberated a little by his absence, I had known some moments of courage. Fortified by the ideological ferment in which we swam in Baku, I dared to sport on my lapel an enamel brooch bearing the image of Lenin. My audacity was short-lived; I was told it was indecent for the daughter of an imprisoned father to wear the portrait of another father, that of the revolution, the main instigator of this incarceration and all the evils afflicting our family. I ended up unpinning the image of Lenin from my breast and returning to the old camp. I was not cut from the same cloth as La Pasionaria.

*

Overwhelmed by the rapid succession of intense emotions and impressions that bombarded me throughout that day, one of the most memorable of my life, I couldn't get to sleep on my first Parisian night. I felt that a sense of frivolity had dominated those hours, with Shamsi's mocking spirit setting the tone. We joked a great deal, we discussed fashions, shopping, the theatre, we gossiped nineteen to the dozen, talking about who had said what, who had slept with whom. The beautiful apartment, my stepmother's elegance, the tutor and the two servants created an air of ease and comfort that I had forgotten and which made a striking contrast with the general upheaval of the years spent 'over there'. How to skip between the ruins of one world and the buildings of another? How to talk about outfits when one has nothing to wear? How to take an interest in someone's lovers when one is trying to get someone else out of prison? The shops were empty, the power went off when one needed it most, ominous rumours poisoned a life already full of real poisons.

Three months earlier I had still been living on another planet, between my Islamic family, jealous of its age-old traditions but already condemned, and the calls of the revolution. For I had heard those calls—a little more courage and I would have gone the other way at the fork in the road.

Here I was in another world, whose charming frivolity brought about a radical change in me after the exhausting seriousness of revolutionary ferment. Here I was experiencing for myself the wonderful diversity of the earth with its surfeit of suffering, pleasure, death and life; I tried to imagine the millions, billions of destinies that intersected on its surface; and as I tried to imagine the unimaginable, I was gripped by an intense desire to live, to burn, to walk through fire, to drink at every spring, poisoned or not.

This fanciful thirst for life plunged me into a fear of growing old which had haunted me off and on for several years. I wasn't yet twenty but every day, every hour, I was getting older as surely as I was breathing. I saw myself as a mature lady watching for the appearance of wrinkles that would dig into my skin with the lightest of touches, at first imperceptible, then with more pressure. My teeth would turn yellow and fall out, my sight would fail, my hair would turn white, I would stop being a woman in the full sense of the word and love would flee from me. And yet love, this sublime, heart-breaking affair, hadn't it already broken my heart? It had already scarred my short life: love lost with Massarin, love submitted to elsewhere with revulsion and refusal. At the thought of seeing Jamil on some ill-fated day, I sat up straight in bed as though afflicted by an unbearable pain. Then I burst into tears, silent lest I wake Zuleykha, who must be dreaming of José, with whom she knew the happiness of love shared. Did she appreciate the value of her good fortune?

I wept for myself, but also for him, my husband, my involuntary torturer, whom in turn I tortured too, reluctantly. We were both victims—but I am repeating myself. And I resumed my litany: it was neither his fault nor mine, but I could not love him, I could only hate him.

That first night in Paris spent in joy and uncertainty, in great hopes and doubt, still seems to me today to have presaged my entire life.

*

The next day, the radical transformation of my person began. I greeted my stepmother in her bed, where, prettily bedecked, she was taking breakfast. Running her hand through my hair and across my cheeks, she gave a dejected sigh: 'Oh, it's all so Baku!'

In her eyes Baku must have represented all that was bad, except for the oil wells which had their uses. But as for the rest! She had always disliked and feared this partly oriental city, populated with natives whom she considered—not always wrongly—savages. What could she do among her in-laws, who were wedded to an aggressive traditionalism, narrower than the neck of a bottle? She too was born into a Muslim family, but since her childhood had lived in Moscow where her father was an engineer, where she went to school and saw virtually only Russians, which made her eager to assimilate, where nothing, other than a theoretical religion, distinguished her from a true Russian.

In Azerbaijan and its capital Baku she had found a part of the Russian Empire that had nothing Russian about it. Its pronounced ethnic and religious particularism was bound to displease her. Had she married my father solely out of self-interest? I don't know. My father cut a fine figure and was handsome in an oriental way. If she had married him for money she had made a mistake, for reasons that everyone now knows but no one foresaw. If emigration had freed her from the Family, it was soon to imprison her in a poverty that would lead to an even more wretched fate, towards a terrible end of life. But no one had an inkling of any of this on that beautiful summer's day when she took it upon herself to drive out the oriental girl and replace her with a fashionable Parisienne.

She scrutinized me as though judging my possibilities and what she could make of me.

'You're so Baku,' she repeated, and I felt myself at fault, all the more readily since I had never appreciated my physique. It wasn't to my taste. I was not 'my type'.

'Take her straight to the hairdresser's,' she said to Zuleykha. My sister dragged me to Rue de Passy where a determined young man set to work after a brief consultation with her. Unbelievably dexterous, he let fly at my head, which emerged from his hands rounded, a fringe above my eyes, the image of a revived Joan of Arc, already a little French.

'Very good,' Amina said approvingly on my return. 'That's already a slight improvement. I've got several dresses ready for you, but first put on this corset, and if it pinches you a little at first, too bad…'

'*Pour être belle, il faut souffrir*. Beauty requires suffering,' Zuleykha interjected sententiously in French.

'That's true. Your hips and that derrière cannot remain at liberty.'

The corset did not pinch me; it suffocated me, strangled me, oppressed me, made me understand by analogy the Chinese tradition of foot-binding. What to do? We were victims of the obsession of that era's elegant ladies: reducing the figure to look like a plank of wood, where the slightest protuberance was a matter of scandal. I walked stiffly and with difficulty in that carapace of iron.

They made me abandon my suit, which I had eagerly purchased in Constantinople in order to surprise the Parisian world with my elegance. As anticipated, it did surprise, but not in the desired sense. I struggled to put on the dress that Amina had chosen for me from her wardrobe. Despite their compressed state, my hips resisted. I thought the dress too plain; I would have preferred it embellished with ruffles, lace or at least buttons. It was straight, bare, monastic, and black too. I did not at all like the Joan of Arc staring defiantly back at me in the long mirror.

My Turkish head covering was lying on the chest of drawers.

'That horror!' Amina cried. 'Don't think you're going to wear it in Paris!'

'It would be funny to take her to the Dôme got up in that.'

Zuleykha and my stepmother burst out laughing, though the name meant nothing to me.

I didn't know that the Dôme was a large cafe, the soul of a Montparnasse of which I had only a vague idea, but I felt stabbed to the quick: were my *charchaf* and I so grotesque that we would make people laugh in that unknown place?

'And like that too—barefaced,' Zuleykha went on.

'Yes, we must teach her to apply make-up.'

They pushed me towards the dressing table, made me sit and let loose on my face: rouge on my cheeks, blue on my eyelids, mascara on my lashes, and then cream and then a huge cloud of powder. Their intentions were good. I knew they wanted to improve my appearance, but was the mask that the mirror showed me still me? I looked like an Easter egg with a funereal touch, thanks to the black fringe. Despair gave me the courage to protest.

'Provincial!' cried Zuleykha. 'You looked as though you'd been through a wringer or a mortal illness. Now your face is alive. You want to look like a little Tolstoyan, but we're in Paris now.'

'I look awful.'

'Provincial, provincial,' Zuleykha repeated. 'And she wants to live in Europe.'

Yes, I wanted to live in Europe, even disfigured. That first day I avoided mirrors, glass and polished surfaces.

Visiting that afternoon, Maryam approved of my metamorphosis, which she proclaimed 'admirable'.

'You're someone else completely. But there's still those eyebrows. Leave them to me.'

She took out of her bag a pair of tweezers, which she was never without. Ever the adversary of abundant follicles, and ours were, God knows, she would pluck them out with furious determination. She even plucked them—a unique procedure as far as I'm aware—from her forearms and her armpits. Every superfluous hair was her personal enemy, whom she had to slay on the spot.

Usually gentle and amenable, she became implacable before my eyebrows. She bent my head back, lent over my forehead and tore out the hairs with remarkable speed and precision. I yelled, my eyes filled with tears, but she continued her work, punctuating it with, 'There, there, I'll be finished soon. It will all be over soon.'

I emerged from her clutches, the skin around my eyebrows on fire, oozing a few small drops of blood. Maryam was satisfied, I was crushed. It had been too much for one day.

She lived in a furnished apartment on Rue Massenet, ten minutes' walk from ours. When they arrived in Paris, Shamsi had rented a sumptuous apartment, but as their funds dwindled they moved to a less sumptuous apartment, and then to a third, much less sumptuous, the one on Rue Massenet. It was the classic émigré process of a gradual descent, if not into hell, at least down the scale of luxury. My parents were on the same path. At the start, when my father was still a minister in a free Azerbaijan and still in possession of his fortune, Amina had rented an extremely luxurious apartment on the Champs-Élysées. When the Bolsheviks occupied Baku and imprisoned my father, she moved to a small private hotel on Rue de la Pompe. Most recently, when everything had turned bad, and the Bolsheviks stubbornly remained in power, she had moved to the apartment on Rue Louis-Boilly, still luxurious. It was the last to be so, as it marked the beginning of the end: one more year of respite and the descent would be complete.

A few days after I arrived Zuleykha took me to see José, who lived in a painter's studio on Rue Jean-Boileau. At that time the street still had an almost rural appearance, with its empty plots and small houses surrounded by gardens. One entered through a porte cochère topped with a sign reading 'Joinery, Cabinet-Making' into a courtyard permeated with the scent of sawdust and timber. The grating of saws and planes and the taps of a hammer could be heard from a shed at the back. On the right, a small building leant against the neighbouring house. Here was José's studio, all in glass. Without bothering to knock—wasn't she at home, after all?—my sister pushed open the door, which José never locked, and went inside. I followed her, consumed with curiosity and eager to be initiated into an artist's life of which I had only the vaguest idea, and over which the fear of unknown devilry hovered.

I had a rude shock as I entered a bizarre universe. The disorder was cosmic: bric-a-brac covered in a thick layer of dust, dozens of tubes of paint scattered all over, canvases, dozens of them too, cluttering the floor or propped against furniture or easels, which stood like guillotines in the four corners of the vast studio; other canvases hung on the walls, covering them entirely. A huge drawing board on trestles took up a large part of the free space in the workshop, so manoeuvring between the board, the canvases and the furniture was no easy task. Much later when I visited the flea market, I saw the resemblance to the picturesque jumble of José's workshop, where a hot water bottle with its neck held together by a substantial quantity of string lay next to a marvellous sabre from a Castilian ancestor stuck in a coal scuttle; there were empty bottles scattered among clothes, an alabaster vase with three fading red roses next to a guitar with a string missing, etc. etc. etc. Over everything hung a scent made up of dust, oil paint and coffee, which José had brewed for us.

My future brother-in-law was standing in the middle of this perfect bohemian scene, palette in his left hand, paint brush in his right, dressed in thick corduroy trousers covered in stains and a (clean) white shirt open to reveal a hairy chest. He had the longest head imaginable; a huge, very white, very serene forehead; elongated eyes framed by long, straight lashes like those of a horse. In profile he resembled the Egyptians in ancient frescoes, with his skull, wasp waist and very broad shoulders.

His inner portrait: a child's cheerfulness, a camel driver's crudeness, and kindness combined with considerable fierceness. At first I was disconcerted by his, one might say, free use of language, his nonchalance, his ingrained bohemian habits that did not prevent him from displaying perfect manners when the circumstances required. And he was a good man, obliging, often funny, with a smile to disarm the devil himself. I was so impressed by his status as an artist, that in my eyes the dust in the studio shimmered in all the colours of the rainbow and the filth on his baggy trousers seemed to symbolize his boundless originality as a PAINTER. I was ready to see cleanliness and tidiness as superfluous, an opinion that I later revised, when I knew artists who were committed to both.

He put down his palette and paint brush, which, when I picture him today, were an integral part of his person, and came over to examine me in detail as though I were a mule for sale, and pronounced with satisfaction: 'She's fine.' Then he launched straight into a venomous domestic tirade aimed at Zuleykha. I realized later that these abrupt changes of mood were typical of him; like a child, he would switch from tears to laughter and back again.

'Well!' he shouted loudly, banging the wooden table where a motley collection of objects jumped in fright. 'Well, when are you going to talk to your father, damn it? My family is as good as yours and better. I'm an hidalgo, not some lousy oilman like you lot.'

I was shocked at his violence and this dismissive reference to our former state.

'You know very well it's not about that. It's about religion.'

'I don't give a tinker's cuss, my darrling,' (he always rolled the R) 'my family is as Catholic as yours is Muslim, and do you think my poor mother' (he couldn't mention his mother without prefixing her with 'poor', perhaps because she was a widow) 'will perform acts of thanksgiving' (I didn't know what that meant) 'when I present to her a'—he hesitated, weighing his words, perhaps out of respect for me—'a foreigner? And I expect you to make the same sacrifice.'

I took a malicious pleasure in the supercilious Zuleykha being taken down a peg or two by her fiery lover. It was a delicious sight. So she too was afraid of facing up to my father, for all her haughty airs designed to confound us. She was trying to look disdainful and to get a word in between José's outbursts, when he had to pause for breath.

'What sailor's language! In our circles—'

'What circles? You've got the manners of savages, from what you've told me. I'm warning you, my darrling, I can't put up with your dithering any longer! It's me or him. Time to choose!'

This formal notice of a choice between love and duty ruled out any further polemic. The topic was exhausted. José poured himself a glass of red wine and knocked it back in one. Convinced and conquered by this proof of José's commitment, Zuleykha gave a final sigh and said, 'I promise to speak to my father tomorrow, or the day after tomorrow—well, at the end of the week,' she added prudently.

Revived by this promise, and perhaps the wine, José leapt to join my sister on the couch and, enthusiastically, they created an amorous scene. They kissed passionately, as though I wasn't there, until a gesture from José made me fear the worst: like Dinarzade in *The Thousand and One Nights*, would I have to be present as they consummated their love? Panicked, I rose, ready to hide, if not under the couch in question, then at least under the table, when Zuleykha said in a languorous voice, 'You can go out for a walk. It's very pretty. Come back in quarter of an hour.'

I made a rush for the door, scandalized and relieved at the same time. Oh, I'd had enough of the bohemian life with all its shamelessness, with all its scorn for convention! As I closed the door, I heard Zuleykha call after me, this time in a more alert voice, a woman who kept her head in all circumstances, 'And don't get lost. Remember the number of the house.'

For the first time in my life I was alone on a street in Paris. It was indeed pretty, with its low houses and gardens like real country gardens, full of trees and warbling birds who were Parisians too, after all. It was hard to believe I was in the great capital. I was moved by the tree-covered bowers behind the railings, by the groves of lilac trees already past their best, by the grass which grew here without any artificial irrigation. It all heralded a future happiness so extraordinary that it couldn't be expressed in words, as it had no name, as I didn't know what it would be.

The little country street took me to a great artery of the great city, strangely cut off in the middle by a viaduct with arches. I stopped, looked left and right and said to myself, 'Whether you go this way or that, whether you go forwards or back, you'll still be in Paris.' A train thundered over the viaduct; cars passed in front of me; a small girl stopped next to me, a basket of flowers in her hand which she was offering to passers-by. I would have liked to buy some in my spirit of celebration, but I didn't have any money. I had yet to see and hold in my hand those coins bearing the image of Marianne. And what need had I of money? It didn't feature in my dreams of Wonderland, where I rose above material considerations.

A quarter of an hour had passed on my first solitary stroll through Paris, which I would never forget. I had to interrupt it and made a slow, reluctant return to the studio. I was the only one to feel embarrassed, however; José and Zuleykha seemed perfectly at ease, normal in every respect, though with added colour in their cheeks and a sparkle in their eyes. As if to teach me to live, José went straight to the heart of a subject that I wanted to forget. 'It's good to make love,' he said with satisfaction. 'Isn't that so, my darrling?'

Since he had taken possession of my sister, it seemed perfectly natural to him to treat me with the familiarity of a brother.

My embarrassment evaporated. 'Oh no,' I cried emphatically, with the full force of my conviction.

José seemed upset. 'Is she mad?' he asked Zuleykha.

'She's young,' my sister replied condescendingly. 'When she's my age…' She sighed beneath the weight of her twenty-two years.

I was infuriated by the conversation, which I found awkward and unpleasant. Casting a reproving look at José, I said, 'I see you haven't made love to my husband.'

'Oh, I wouldn't have done that. I don't like men; well, not in that way. Did he make a pig's ear of it?'

A pig's ear—this abstruse language went over my head. When he realized this he added, 'Well, I mean, did he do it like an ox?'

I had no idea about the sexual conduct of oxen, but this time I grasped his meaning.

'I don't know. But it was revolting. I don't want any more of it.'

My childhood guide in these delicate matters, my cousin Gulnar, with her brilliant insights into the act of love, had told me so much about it that I had been expecting indescribable ecstasy. Alas, this act, which I first experienced at the age of fifteen in the arms of a hated husband, disgusted and disappointed me so much that it took me years to put it behind me.

I was expecting mockery, instead of which José came over and tapped me on the cheek with a paternal air. 'It really is very good, my darrling. Chastity too is very fine.'

He then held forth on the life of a Teresa of Ávila, a lady I'd never heard of but whom he held in high regard, both for her gifts as a writer and her way of serving God in the most absolute purity.

She was the daughter of a Castilian hidalgo, like José himself. She entered a convent—this is where their paths diverged—and went on to reform it, as she found it too frivolous for her liking.

I realized then what was later confirmed—that José was an advocate of chastity for his female relatives and loved them to be virtuous. He spoke with pride of his 'poor mother', who was widowed young and did not remarry on principle, and of his sister Anna-Maria, widowed at forty and destined to remain so. They were exemplary women, models to follow. As he already saw me as his sister-in-law, he sincerely encouraged my purity. He himself had given up on it for obvious reasons: because he was a man, and his virility, impossible to subdue, led him in every direction. He was an artist too and art obliges—sensuality in all its forms was at his core, one might say. But the freedoms of the artist's life were counterbalanced by his Spanish origins, to which a conquering Moor had perhaps added a grain of rigour concerning women and their virtue. This duality, encountered in many people, was clearly manifested in José, who preached virtue and libertinage with equal eloquence.

From that first meeting on that fine summer's day, José and I became the best of friends and remained so even after he and my sister divorced a dozen years later. Another couple who in their early days called to mind Goethe's words, 'All beginnings are delightful,' but who would gradually unravel until the final destruction. I was perhaps wrong to mention it here.

*

Zuleykha could not bring herself to take the great leap into the unknown. It was easier to make promises, feign bravado and criticize the cowardice of others than to face defeat and the wrath of our father. Another equally unpleasant possibility presented itself: the pain that a marriage flouting all his beliefs, all our traditions, might cause our father. He had already suffered ruin, imprisonment and exile at an advanced age. This was in the past, but what did the present have to offer? A future without prospects, maybe terminal exile, maybe poverty. Would he now have to bear this ordeal too?

I could hear Zuleykha, who usually slept like a log, tossing and turning in bed, sighing and sometimes crying. I felt sorry for her. She had to face José's impatience, which was taking on dangerous proportions. He was threatening to break it off, was planning a long trip to Spain, and maybe wouldn't return. He was bluffing, and Zuleykha knew it, but she also knew that poker players don't bluff all the time. We had all been initiated into the game in childhood and knew this danger.

After every scene of threats reinforced with imprecations, she would part from José firmly resolved to make the great leap, but as soon as she reached home some obstacle would arise, most of the time thanks to an obliging imagination, and it would all begin again.

The lovers procrastinated indefinitely from summer into autumn, my first autumn in Paris. In the Parc de la Muette the leaves turned gold and red and fell in undulating waves onto the earth, covering it in a carpet finer than those of the orient. The children playing in the park were wrapped in woollens. The mornings grew fresher, the sun rose later, and Zuleykha also delayed taking her decisive leap.

Then José dropped a bombshell. He was unfaithful to my sister, or at least claimed to have been; there were, thank God, plenty of women who knew how to live. Having made this observation, he used the crudest language to suggest that Zuleykha 'go and get fucked somewhere else'. As this wasn't what she wanted at all, she shed a torrent of tears, railed against José's vile behaviour, hinted at a possible suicide, but the only effect was to strengthen his irrevocable decision. She knew she would have to act if she wanted to keep him.

She returned home, drank some strong alcohol in the study for courage, swallowed two tablets of a celebrated pick-me-up and headed for the drawing room, her steps still hesitant. My father was alone at a table, enjoying his favourite occupation: playing patience. She stumbled in the doorway, I don't know whether from alcohol or fear, but maintained her dignity. She didn't close the door properly and I shamelessly made the most of it, taking up a strategic position where I could not only hear but also see part of the spectacle to come.

My father did not even look at Zuleykha when, more dead than alive, she perched on the edge of a chair opposite him. He was preoccupied with a thorny problem in his game of patience. Imposing and phlegmatic as always, he moved the cards laid out before him with an absorbed air. A few moments flew by in silence. With one finger, Zuleykha showed my father a move he had missed. I knew she was letting herself become engrossed in the game. That's that, I said to myself, another failure.

But love, which is said to be stronger than death, also proved itself stronger than patience. Zuleykha looked up and said in a voice choked with emotion, 'Papa—'

'What now?' he groaned, looking up at his daughter too. He was expecting another move to complete the game. She dropped her eyes before his gaze, then, trembling with fear, rattled out the words that were to change the face of the world, that she had suppressed for months: 'I would like to marry a Spanish painter. He's Catholic.'

And then my father gave the simplest, most astonishing reply in the world. 'Well, who's stopping you?'

He had spoken gruffly, but humour had filtered through. He understood full well his daughter's state of mind. Having spoken, he continued to move the cards calmly, gravely, reflectively.

Zuleykha stared at him dumbfounded, mouth open. She had considered every eventuality except this one. She continued to stare at my father. He continued to focus on his cards. The minutes continued to pass. The game of patience hadn't worked out, so my father could devote himself to secondary matters.

'What a silly ass you are! Did you think I was going to kill you because you want to marry a Christian?'

He mixed the cards, put them into a pile, shuffled the pack, and started to lay them out on the table in the hallowed order. Do you know what my idiot of a sister did next? She cried. She cried, I think, from relief and emotion, and from gratitude, to be sure. Perhaps also from regret at having suffered so much for nothing and having been so unfairly cheated on by José.

'Oh, Papa, I was so afraid to talk to you.' Her voice was barely audible.

'You halfwit, do you think I'm frozen in the past, attached to things that have detached themselves from us? Of course I would have liked to stay in Baku, to see you all married to Muslims, our own kind, whose mothers and fathers we know. I would have liked to keep our fortune, and especially to die there, to die where our fathers died and are buried. This was not Allah's wish and He alone decides.'

He carefully studied the cards he had just laid out to assess his chances of winning the game. Then he asked, 'What's he like?'

Zuleykha, who was still wiping her eyes and blowing her nose, immediately recovered her spirits and her epic sense of exaggeration, and became dangerously eloquent in singing

José's praises. I say 'dangerously', because painting someone in vivid colours risks doing them a disservice, especially if the gap between description and reality is wide.

'Oh, Papa, he's so handsome and so intelligent and so cultured and so good and he loves me so much it's practically idolatry' (I felt she was overdoing it) 'and he has a philosopher's forehead and he recites Villon like no one else you know Villon is a great medieval poet he's a poet himself and he will be a good husband and a great painter of course in the style of Goya or Velásquez more Goya and he loves you and respects you as a son and he's already oriental in many respects because of the Moors you know they ruled Spain for such a long time and he loves the oriental music sung by the Gypsies and he loves the Moorish style because of the Alhambra you know he is really very Muslim at heart in many ways and you know he is from an hidalgo family a very good family and if Shamsi is scornful don't believe him you know he's an unbearable snob and if he tells you that José is no one I can tell you that José is from a better family than ours well if one is being prejudiced but neither you nor I are like that and we laugh at the nobility your father was a peasant and what matters is the heart and José has a heart of gold and he is generous even though he's poor but he won't be for long he's the new Goya he will make a lot of money and he's just sold two canvases.'

Zuleykha would have continued this speech at lightning speed without any punctuation, as life was too beautiful to linger over such trifles, for a good ten minutes more, were it not for the annoying need to breathe in order to survive. She broke off, out of breath, and sought the approval of the Supreme Judge. The Supreme Judge bore a dignified expression worthy of his office.

'Well, if a quarter of your hymn of praise is true, I'll be happy. Bring him to meet me whenever you want.'

She leapt up and rushed over to plant a kiss on his cheek with all the effusion one can imagine. My father knitted his thick eyebrows, as he didn't like displays of emotion. As I said, our whole family took a dim view of mawkishness. Perhaps he had frowned for another reason too.

'Wait a minute. You smell of alcohol. That's a fine state of affairs. Marry a Christian if you must, but don't become a drunkard.'

'No no, not at all. It was just to give me courage. I promise…'

She was already sprinting to the door, determined to run straight to José. I just had time to make a speedy getaway.

*

The meeting took place under the best auspices. My father took to him straightaway, as José's behaviour combined the deference towards his elders that was part of his own tradition with cheerfulness and an ability to adapt. This ability was so well developed that soon after joining our family he would arm himself with a dagger and dance with brio what he believed to be a Caucasian dance, and would indignantly tell his friends 'they've taken everything away from us', the plural pronoun referring of course to the Bolsheviks. While his spontaneity and naivety sometimes led to gaffes, he was soon forgiven. He was immediately adopted by all the family, Shamsi excepted, who was scandalized by this union with a Christian, a painter; 'A tramp,' he would say, with the searing contempt that made him so inhuman. My father would dismiss his criticism with a philosophical gesture and a 'Poor fellow, he's very pleasant. And times have changed, after all.'

Shamsi would fulminate. 'Here am I, a bey with x generations of nobility behind me,' (I forget how many) 'now related to that painter and decorator, that uncouth doodler.'

He had forgotten or wanted to forget that he was already related to a family whose line went back as far as a peasant grandfather who couldn't read or write in his native Azeri or in the language of the Russian colonizers. Despite his disdain, he had to meet the painter and decorator, and he haughtily touched his hand rather than shook it. José, always good-natured, pretended not to notice the insult, and with his painter's practised eye admired Shamsi's Mongol cast, comparing him to Tamerlane, a skilful piece of flattery that hit the bull's eye; nothing could please this unbearable snob of a brother-in-law more than a comparison with an illustrious figure. He gave nothing away, but I am sure that, in that very moment, his defences began to weaken.

The marriage was celebrated as soon as José found an even larger studio than the one he already had. It was so huge that it could be divided into several rooms through an ingenious system of partitions the height of a man, which made it easy to communicate without getting up, but had its advantages and disadvantages. This enormous space was heated by a stove, which was enormous too but required renewed labour every morning and the muscles of a stoker. José installed a tub in the toilet and with his customary optimism called it the 'shower room'. For a former petroleum princess the home lacked comfort, never mind luxury, but love substituted for both, for the first few years of marriage at least.

Let's go back to the day of the wedding. It was only a civil ceremony, as the other kind was out of the question. In the eyes of José's very Catholic family, Zuleykha would always remain a concubine, while as far as Islam was concerned this union was a disgrace best passed over in silence. Neither José, who on rare occasions was a believer but usually an atheist, nor Zuleykha, whose religious feelings were vague, seemed to mind. And if we had yet to enter the delights of the permissive society, the effects of the Great War and the October Revolution, the fall of the monarchs after 1918 and the simultaneous rise of democracy, had already acted as a solvent on customs. Fall, rise, progress, regression—opinions differed on the definitions, but the effects were there, eroding traditions if not to say superstitions. Thus, this marriage, inconceivable just a decade ago, could receive my father's blessing, though he was already inclined towards liberalism, as we've seen.

The French state duly married the Spaniard who had come from Castile and the Azerbaijani who had escaped from Baku at the town hall in the sixteenth arrondissement. Afterwards, a disparate crowd gathered for a Spanish-Caucasian lunch at the house. Not all the Muslims in attendance approved of the marriage, but since weddings are in principle happy occasions they celebrated by drinking a great deal, not of the wine forbidden by the Prophet, but of vodka, brandy and other spirits that He had not mentioned, for obvious reasons. They drank far too much, which made them very excitable. They danced with daggers, sang together and made speeches in a free interpretation of French. It was a joy to hear them: one raised his glass to the health of the 'newborns'; another wished them 'eternal velocity' (for which read 'felicity'); a third trembled as he evoked the beautiful 'mixed geniture' that would soon honour the freshly united Caucasus and Spain. It was impossible to stop them; and they weren't in the least bothered if people didn't listen.

The house resembled a madhouse presided over by my father, satisfied and serene, very much the oriental philosopher, as always above the fray. Shamsi, distant and contemptuous, drank a lot too, but he could take his drink and did not slip from his haughty dignity. Zuleykha was decked out in all the colours of the rainbow, the most daring earrings and a beatific smile, which revealed glimpses of the tip of her tongue. According to the ever spiteful Shamsi, she resembled the Gruyère advertisement with its 'laughing cow' slogan, which was on the walls of Paris at the time and has now returned after a long absence, not to the walls, but to those familiar round boxes. My sister was careful not to drink in my father's presence, but knocked it back when she was out of his sight.

As for José, he was well and truly drunk, which made him unsteady on his feet and gave him a tendency to ramble. He repeated feebly, 'Zulu, the Old Man with the Beard is a... he nearly stopped us getting married...' He was lucid enough to utter this blasphemy out of my father's hearing, who, for all his liberalism, would have taken it badly. Yahweh, the God of the Armies of the Old Testament; the forgiving God of the Christians, who chooses to become incarnate in order to save them; Allah, the Merciful without limits of the Koran, so transcendent that the idea of incarnation horrifies Muslims as much as blasphemy; these three gods of the Book common to the three successive monotheistic religions merged in José's tipsy mind into the Bearded God whose only relations with mankind are threats and interdictions from his throne on high. All the childhood prohibitions in His name must have created a thick layer of resentment in José's subconscious.

His invention of the diminutive 'Zulu' for Zuleykha was unfortunate too, as it reminded the French of an inopportune expedition against the Zulu people during which the son of Napoleon III died, a death that may have changed the history of France. True, only one Frenchman represented our host country at the party, and he was only half-French, his mother being a Georgian princess. Quite inebriated himself, his national pride was doubtless asleep. He too bore a princely title, as a direct descendant of Joachim Murat, something he exulted in, as well he might. Amazingly, he looked like his ancestor, though several generations separated them.

It wasn't until late in the evening that the newlyweds left us in a state that did not bode well for their first night of wedlock.

Glimpses of the Bohemian Life

Zuleykha had tied the knot at last, while I dreamt only of untying it. I received frequent, tearful letters from Constantinople, gloomy missives in which Jamil brought wholly justified grievances against me. As I unfolded the sheet of paper, I would flinch at the mere sight of the handwriting, my reluctance bordering on aversion as a face rose from between the lines that I wished never to see again. The letters rehashed an old story of unrequited love in which one party suffered and the other submitted, with the added resentments particular to our own story, those too entirely justified. Jamil felt abandoned in Constantinople, where he had gone because of me. On his own he would never have left even Bolshevik Baku for this foreign land where he was no one and had nothing: neither family, nor money, nor friends, nor hope of any sort, if I remained absent and unattainable in faraway Paris. His appeals proclaimed his moral and material misery, the unbearable iniquity of his fate in which I was both innocent and responsible. I hated him and pitied him. I resented him for daring to love me, but took pride in making a man suffer like one of those vamps so admired on the silver screen. I was already extremely well acquainted with the contradictions of a divided heart.

Like a condemned prisoner I sweated over my replies to these cries for pity. Without putting it into so many words, I tried to make clear what I had to tell him: that I would not resume a relationship that felt like suicide of body and soul alike.

Amina had told me in confidence (though it was practically an open secret) that my father was aware how disastrous this forced marriage had been for me and was considering the idea of my divorce. The remote possibility was enough to send me wild with hope. Squeezing the tiny Koran in its engraved silver case, which to me was more of a lucky charm than a holy object, I begged Allah to permit this divorce: triumphant liberation for me, sorrow and defeat for Jamil—and the first bad deed of my life, though life had forced it upon me. We were pawns on the chessboard of our fates, he and I, and had been moved without compassion.

*

My family led a novel life for a while longer; novel in that our daily sustenance was provided by a share, difficult to determine, of a pearl. Let me explain: my father had just sold a necklace of pearls of great price and the sum raised had bailed us out for a while, allowing us a way of life without regard for the future, which my father preferred to forget for the time being, relying as always on Allah, who alone makes and breaks fortunes, who decides them in advance, thereby rendering all our turmoil pointless. His main occupation was the card table, where he laid out his games of patience, devoting many hours and all his attention to them. When necessary he would cheat himself to make the game come out: dishonesty that I disapproved of in silence, as I didn't dare accuse him openly.

Amina's occupations were much more varied but just as futile, and they cost money, an accusation that could not be laid against the games of patience, free of charge as they were. She went to the hairdresser and to dressmakers and played mahjong, which was fashionable at the time, with a bevy of (still) elegant ladies, all formerly wealthy like us, and though émigrés and ruined (still) leading the idle life of 'over there'.

My half-brother was shooting up under the watchful eye of his tutor who, despite his age and subordinate position, dared to show an interest in me that I found shocking. He kept telling me about his dreams, in which I played far too great a role for my liking. These were passing irritations that I soon forgot, happy to wake every morning in Paris and to have recovered my status as a young girl, more evident since Zuleykha's marriage. I would serve tea to the ladies gathered around the card table, pick up their handkerchiefs, find their handbags, listen to their chatter during breaks in the game. Little by little I became accustomed to their frivolity, which I'd found shocking at first.

My greatest pleasure was my Sunday visits to the Josézous, my invented name for them. There, I received my initiation into the bohemian lifestyle with its dual attractions that I would pursue and relish all my life: freedom and fantasy.

A baroque world, charming and slightly mad, had formed around them. Whoever visited returned. Tower of Babel, cluttered chaos, artist's studio, society salon, imaginary bullring, place of business—they did interior decorating to make ends meet—their house was one or more of these things at any one time. Various Western languages were spoken there, and other, rarer ones too, such as our mother tongue, Azeri, or Chechen or Georgian, all three of them Caucasian. Laughter, conversation, disagreements came one after the other or all at once. Quarrels between our hosts were often vicious, since both were afflicted with fiery tempers.

The chaos was almost as great as in José's bachelor studio, despite the efforts of Zuleykha, who with an optimism undaunted by the facts pursued first of all the dust, second José's belongings scattered on every available surface, and third mice of an especially shrewd variety well equipped for the struggle for existence. Through the most ingenious manoeuvres they enjoyed with impunity the bait on the snap traps, and got inside the box traps to gobble up the morsels of bacon José had put there, emerging with head held high. Crunching poisoned crumbs did no harm whatsoever to their health. It took three large, fat, contemptuous cats to get rid of them. All neutered, they were spoilt, caressed and adored, but by no means led a parasitic life, since they posed as models as well as hunted. The Josézous treated them with such respect that they always addressed them formally, and did not like anyone to be familiar towards them. 'How can you not respect their dignity?' they would ask.

Some of the less well-off regulars envied the cats their lifestyle, especially in respect of nutrition. In particular Ivan Petrovich, an émigré (Russian, of course, as one can tell from his name) who was idle, lazy, fond of the bottle and managed to live the life of a parasite, and on credit too. He was the greatest liar in Paris, endowed with a jovial nature and a wonderful imagination that would have delighted many a novelist. Was

Einstein the topic of conversation? Ivan Petrovich would launch into a detailed account of a lunch during which he had once astonished the scientist with his knowledge of mathematics. Was Trotsky the topic of conversation? Ivan Petrovich hinted at a mysterious encounter with the great revolutionary who made the mistake of disregarding his advice, a blunder that would cost him dear. When a hunter boasted of the number of pheasants or, worse still, hares he had shot during his last hunt in the Sologne, Ivan Petrovich would give a condescending smile and describe his bear hunts in the Siberian forests, where he had on occasion risked his life finishing off the beast with his bare hands.

A marvellous raconteur and first-class mimic, he possessed such powers of suggestion that he could win over the most sceptical listener, at least for a while. The certain knowledge that he was lying did not diminish the pleasure of listening to him, though his audience might make fun of him once the spell was broken. Tall, blonde, expressive blue eyes looking all around, he would embellish his tale with astounding impressions and spot-on imitations: he would become celebrities whom he seemed to know intimately; he would whistle like a train, sing like a bird, cough like a consumptive, bellow like a bear. He was tremendous fun and most people didn't mind his sponging, for all the pleasure he gave. I should make clear in passing that parasitism is a Russian institution as old as the kingdom of the tsars, a tradition, moreover, richly reflected in Russian literature. How has a sociologist not yet written a thesis on this subject, which is so typical of Holy Russia and doubtless a product of the country's history? It would be interesting to know if this tradition still persists.

I should mention that the Josézous's studio was a separate building inside a courtyard, with no immediate neighbours; hence the opportunity to make a racket even late into the night without causing a 'breach of the peace', to use that ambiguous legal formula.

The Josézous loved to hold parties in the splendid isolation of this island on Sundays. Everyone would contribute what they could, but admission was possible without payment too. Live and let live was the order of the day. In this atmosphere, everyone enjoyed every freedom as long as it didn't impinge on the freedom of others. And isn't that the definition of freedom? The guests drank, ate, debated and danced with the passion of youth and exotic temperaments prone to excess of all kinds. We couldn't get away without a bullfight, almost as noisy as a real one. José and his poet cousin Almeria would get thoroughly worked up and have terrible rows about the execution of one pass or another. Almeria, small and thin with smouldering eyes and lively gestures, would tear the red cloth representing the cape from José's grasp, and cry, rolling his Rs like thunder, 'You bumpkin. You'rrre going to get yourrrself gorrred,' then execute the relevant pass with exquisite grace. Piqued, José would mutter Franco-Spanish insults, but Almeria would hear nothing in the throes of his passion and pursue the bull with the fervour that made him exceptional, like the hero of a novel.

Slovenly in appearance and none too clean, he lived in a fantasy world where material concerns were lost in the ether. Did he ever wash? Did he eat only in other people's homes? Were his ID papers his only possessions? He spent his nights either writing alone (obviously) in his room, or with friends, drinking and talking, unconcerned whether anyone was listening. Talking was more important to him than eating. His brain was so crammed with contradictory ideas that it would burst under the pressure, finding relief in a torrent of words that would pour out until every subject had been exhausted. And since Almeria was well read, the list of subjects was not soon exhausted.

Love was his great hobby horse. He always spoke with pathos, but when he talked of love, his voice became even more tragic. He complained of the indifference of women whose attitude, he said, denied his very existence. 'They do not see me, not even when they look into my eyes.' He quivered with ardour, anticipating love, which always escaped him, and would curse his futile passion. Futile? Wouldn't it be better if he expressed all this vain activity in his poems, the very essence of his life?

I bumped into him on the street one day. As though sleepwalking, he was conversing with himself, making grand, eloquent gestures, enveloped in that air of madness typical of people who talk to themselves. I tried to avoid him, but he suddenly snapped out of his dream and saw me. It was our first meeting on our own. I was caught in a trap, but without the shrewdness of the mice in the Josézous's studio. I spent an unpleasant quarter of an hour listening to his vehement reproaches: I didn't see him either, I denied his existence like all the other women, and this non-existence was tantamount to death. The man frightened me. He was a Dostoevskyan character going to waste, as there was no author to make use of him.

*

The Josézous's great cosmopolitan entourage even included some French people, though the Spanish-Caucasian-Russian element held sway. I have already mentioned Michel Murat, descendant of Joachim, who was only half-French, the other half coming from a Georgian princess. Another Frenchman, the Baron of Berwick, also boasted a glorious lineage: he was descended from James Stuart, Duke of Berwick, James II of England's illegitimate son, who became a Marshal of France. He had a rare, luminous first name—Hélion—and was handsome, with a passion for amateur dramatics. As a result, we were often treated to performances of the classics in which he played the lead roles alongside his mistress, who had been an actress in her youth and who cheered us immensely with her rather old-fashioned refinement and prudishness. My brother-in-law loved crude, risqué jokes, whose effect on her gave us much delight. She would gasp in shock, crying 'For pity's sake, José!' and blushing a genuine crimson, and would get up as though to run out but then sit back down again. She always returned to these gatherings, which had no equal.

Thanks to the influx during this great era of emigration, there was no shortage of titled people, or commoners who were nonetheless well known, such as Ivan Shchukin, son of an extremely rich Moscow merchant and celebrated art collector, who had been one of the first to discover the Impressionists and buy their work practically wholesale. We called him by the diminutive 'Vanichka'. Having grown up amid the wonders of art, Vanichka had acquired a remarkable erudition and gave us veritable lectures on pictorial art, which we listened to with rapt attention.

A brilliant tsarist general, covered in medals and so handsome that he had become a dancer in a Russian nightclub, enchanted us with songs from the depths of his native Georgia in the days when it was still a great kingdom and neighbour of Byzantium. Tzavidze had fought in the White armies in Siberia and lost his wife and child in the unspeakable chaos of the civil war, a tragedy that befell hundreds of thousands of soldiers and civilians. Prematurely white, this only made him more seductive, with his eyes that shone like lanterns, his fine, straight nose, his noble bearing and his Georgian features. He spoke Russian with a Georgian accent, exactly the same as his formidable compatriot Dzhugashvili, alias Stalin. Accompanying himself on the guitar, he sang songs of unbearable sadness, then would overcompensate, as psychologists might say, cutting loose in a wave of gaiety bordering on insanity. Malicious tongues said he was irredeemably stupid, which did not prevent his being picked up and married by an American millionairess whom he had whisked across the dance floor in his nightclub, then seduced. His success owed as much to his title as to his looks—he was a prince, like most of the Georgian émigrés.

I won't describe all the unusual characters who visited the Josézous, most of them living on the fringes of society, unable to join a specific social group for reasons of either character or circumstances beyond their control, as the phrase has it. Where does the charm of a book come from? Where does the charm of a person come from? Where does the charm of a house come from? Without doubt the appeal of the Josézous's house came from them most of all, and then from this picturesque carousel of characters who revolved around them, disparate in terms of culture, religion and country, but creating nonetheless a delicious whole.

My brother-in-law Shamsi dubbed them a 'gaggle of wretches', or 'painters and decorators', who in the olden days would have been confined to the outbuildings of stately homes. He did not deign to attend. Had he forgotten the fall of the nobility, and his own too? No, but he considered it temporary; it would end when Russia rose from its ashes. An event that I for one had no desire to see. Rather than oil wells, Islam and the Caucasus, I chose the enchantment of Paris and the magic of freedom, though I didn't know then that it was itself often melancholic. I wasn't yet free but knew that I would be, one day. In the meantime I lived through fantasies which filled the void in my heart, and revelled vicariously in the life of an artist.

*

My taste of the artistic life was not limited to the gatherings at the Josézous. We would venture up to the pinnacle of international bohemia, the crowning glory that was the Dôme-Rotonde-Coupole trinity; I say 'venture up', although geographically speaking we ventured down from the sixteenth arrondissement to the plain of Montparnasse, which teemed with an extraordinary mass of humanity, responsible in large part for the label *'Années folles'* or Crazy Years, given to the period stretching from the end of the First World War to the Great Depression of 1929–30.

We didn't know then that it would one day have this appellation, but our small circle lived up to the name, having a riotous time in the heart of the trinity, so famous around the world that tourists came by the coachload, a stop as obligatory as Versailles, the Sacré-Cœur or the Louvre.

What do I see, when I recall the years 1925–26–27? If I close my eyes and open the floodgate to memory, I see a terrace even larger than the interior of the cafe to which it belongs, in this case the Rotonde, José's preferred venue as the Iberian contingent there was particularly large. I can see a sea of heads and shoulders gathered around pedestal tables cluttered with cups, glasses and bottles; I can hear a garbled buzz that serves as background noise to the cries, shouts, laughter, the 'hello', 'zdravstvuyte', 'buongiorno', 'guten Tag', etc. etc. All the languages of the world, including even French, mixed together in this multinational cocktail. The painter Guy Arnoux was said to have hung a tricolour above his doorway with the inscription 'French Consulate', for the benefit of French people feeling out of place in this 'every man's land'.

Highly sociable and approachable, José would rather too often get into conversation with strangers, who would converge at our table and want to buy him a drink. While he knew a crowd of Spaniards, Zuleykha knew a crowd of Russians, most of them painters—Yakovlev, Goncharova, Larionov, Annenkov, Shukhayev, etc.—who preferred to paint in post-war Paris rather than in Russia, which had just about recovered from the Civil War, but not from the evils it had caused.

Does anyone still remember that before the White émigrés invaded, Montparnasse experienced another invasion, that of the Reds, whose names were later to become famous: Trotsky, Lunacharsky, Ilya Ehrenburg and especially, especially, the most famous of all, Lenin? For the sake of historical accuracy, I should make clear that rather than the cafes of Montparnasse, he frequented the Bibliothèque nationale, cycling in the early morning from one end of Paris to another, as he lived on Rue Marie-Rose. His apartment there is now a museum, with period furniture and a wretched little sink, where one washed in turn one's body, one's laundry and one's crockery—providing a better illustration than any long dissertation of the progress, at least in terms of material comfort, between then and now. For the house that he occupied, while not luxurious, was in the bourgeois style, whereas today we could not imagine an apartment without a bathroom. Lenin settled in Paris for nearly three years because of the high concentration of Russian revolutionaries, who allowed him to labour efficiently towards the fulfilment of all his hopes—but there's no need to spell it out. It was at this time that he wrote the prescient lines, 'It's not possible that the revolutionary proletariat of France, with its astonishing revolutionary traditions, its culture, its spirit of sacrifice, its admirable militancy, should not create a powerful communist party.'

Though he did not often visit the trinity at the heart of Montparnasse, he did sometimes frequent another celebrated cafe nearby, the charming Closerie des Lilas, to play chess. They used to show visitors the table where he would sit to play this game, appreciated by many Russian intellectuals and Russians in general.

If I've digressed from the *Années folles* to recall Lenin, whose image I once bore on my adolescent breast, it's for good historical reasons: how can we forget this émigré from the pre-revolutionary era whose actions led to the influx of White émigrés? Without him this emigration would not have taken place, just as this memoir would not have been written. A mystic once said that God writes straight with curved lines, while his adversary, the Prince of Darkness, seems to write crookedly with crooked lines; hence these convolutions of history, where human reason seems absent.

It is hard to imagine today that in the limited area known as Montparnasse, comprising just the Boulevard Montparnasse and part of the Boulevard Raspail, with their intersecting streets, some of which are well known—Grande-Chaumière, Delambre, Bréa, Stanislas, etc.—in that area of scarcely a few hectares, dozens of future celebrities were concentrated. There's no question of listing them all, but I'll mention a few to jog our memories: among the Americans, for example, the fascinating couple Zelda and Scott Fitzgerald, who personified beauty, talent and drama; Hemingway, Henry Miller, James Joyce and Sylvia Beach, with her bookshop Shakespeare and Company, where all the American elite would congregate; the Russian Slavs and the Russian Jews: Chagall, Kisling, Diaghilev, Stravinsky, Prokofiev, Kuprin, Soutine, etc. Foujita, Modigliani, Moréas, whose real name was Papadiamantópoulos, De Chirico, Picasso, though only rarely did the latter come down from his Montmartre to Montparnasse, etc. Enough. Some of these people of talent or genius have climbed to the heights of achievement, but how many have stagnated in failure and fallen into the abyss? Pascin said that one went to Montparnasse 'to live there and to drop dead there'. And as if to prove his point, he 'dropped dead'—but in Montmartre, committing suicide in a terrible fashion.

Montparnasse used to be countryside, and the Dôme, the first cafe in the Trinity, was just a shack. Knowing what became of this intersection of streets, and of its famous lives, we can only marvel at the metamorphoses that cities, people and nations undergo. We have often wondered why this district experienced what it did, why it acquired legendary status and then became the unremarkable place that it is today. Why did these throngs of feted or failed artists scurry there and not somewhere else? Was it the ready availability of lodgings, which seems impossible today? The cheap lifestyle, which was especially attractive to people on the margins of society? No one knows. We do know, though, that at this Mount Parnassus 'dedicated to Apollo and the Muses' a crowd of creative people revelled, hustled, drank too much, loved, hated, found themselves and lost themselves, and so did mere mortals too, drawn by the fascination that the arts and their imitations have always exerted over the crowd.

All these people lived on hope and cafés crèmes, if not on alcohol, a far more expensive beverage. Great artists at the start of their careers kept body and soul together with this famous 'crème' that came to symbolize a painter's way of life. Zadkine recalls how he and his friend Modigliani would struggle at the end of the month. They both had to rely on their families sending help, one from Smolensk, the other from Livorno. But poverty did not shake their confidence in life. 'We would stroll down to the Vavin crossroads and settle on a terrace, waiting like fishermen for a friend to come and tide us over by lending us the three francs we needed for lunch chez Rosalie.'

This is a distant memory, but I can see clearly the small cafe in the Rue Campagne-Première where José would take us for lunch and where we perhaps, or even certainly, rubbed shoulders with Zadkine and Modigliani. But how did my eye fail to photograph the handsome Italian whose picture I was later to dream over, that youthful Apollo dressed in his velvet suit with 'its mother-of-pearl shimmer acquired from the sun and rain', according to Zadkine? My eyes may have touched this suit— better still, perhaps I also touched this suit, without seeing it;

and this blindness fills me with vexation. How much have we missed for want of discernment?

Many artists went to Italian Rosalie's cafe, because as a former model she had a soft spot for painters and would often feed them on credit. Modigliani is said to have 'foisted' on her whole sketchbooks of drawings, which she threw with scorn and/or annoyance into the cellar, where the rats did their work. What happened to them?

José never asked for credit, and Zuleykha and I could accompany him with heads held high. I wanted to make that clear.

I hope I'll be forgiven another comment on Modigliani, whose horrifying fate has often haunted me. This singular character, an aristocratic Villon transposed into our century, slowly killed himself with alcohol and drugs. His mistress, Jeanne Hébuterne, nicknamed the Angel of Reims, could not face life without her hero. Though pregnant with their second child, she threw herself from a fifth-floor window. This couple offers us two types of suicide: slow and instantaneous. Those who seek non-existence choose one or the other for reasons that are mysterious, sometimes subconscious.

Suicide was common in Montparnasse, where sensitivity, instability and a penchant for alcohol and drugs were widespread. But generalizations always diminish the truth, and artists great and small knew how to maintain their equilibrium. I consider José one of the small artists. He had a surprising equanimity, and was a 'conscious and organized' worker, who faced up to his duties despite the anarchic tastes for which the Spanish are so well known.

As for the major artists, Chagall immediately comes to mind: his capacity for work, his equilibrium, his determined march towards a goal that everything in his early life had obstructed, have always been exemplary. In his autobiography he talks about his childhood, his adolescence, his early days, all difficult. He worked in Montparnasse, in a studio with broken windows, though the rent was no more than thirty-five francs a quarter, which must have warmed his heart in one sense. Even in gold francs, a rent of twelve francs per month for a studio in Montparnasse, even with all its windows broken, sounds to us like a legend of Atlantis drowned by history.

'It was wonderful,' Chagall recalls. 'I worked all night.' While he worked on a canvas by the light of a miserable oil lamp, he would hear from the neighbouring studio the sobs of a badly treated model, arguments, Italian songs. He would hear Soutine returning from Les Halles armed with poultry on the turn, destined for a fine still life.

'The studio hadn't been swept for a week. Frames, eggshells and empty tuppenny pots of broth were scattered over the floor. The light was burning and so was I. I was painting furiously...'

This description brings back images of José's bachelor studio before the advent of Zuleykha; stricken by the same chaos, the same eggshells strewn over the floor. The only difference was the electricity; the oil lamp had had its day.

Chagall's text paints the layperson's image of an artist's life. It has the lot: cold, chaos, a precarious diet, scorn for material concerns and, to top it off, the sacred flame that devours the creator and in the best case becomes his salvation and his triumph. Happy are those crossing the desert for whom a mirage becomes an oasis. Woe betide the failures.

The Montparnasse of tragedy did not exist for the very young Caucasian goose, who did not try to see behind the trappings.

She was happy to sip a drink and let her not so perceptive gaze drift over people and objects alike. It was wonderful just to be part of this lively, colourful scene where all races, nationalities and languages mixed into a bubbling magma. We spent summer evenings there, eating and drinking, listening, watching, greeting and talking to the procession of friends of the Josézous who came one after the other to sit at our table, where the ashtrays overflowed with butts and the crockery formed a growing superstructure with every passing hour.

José used to spend the whole night there drinking and talking, but now that he had domestic responsibilities he would take me back to the roost at a respectable hour, especially if a dubious young man should hover around the Caucasian goose. We've already seen that he did not trifle with the honour of his close relatives, and it never occurred to him to leave me alone in the clutches of a seducer in this place of potential perdition. I was still a long way from my dream of freedom.

After this immersion in the artistic life, I would return to my young girl's bedroom, which sometimes made me forget that I was well and truly married, a forgetfulness that I carefully cultivated. I would diligently resume my daydreaming, which has always been my succour amid the boredom of the everyday and my source of prodigious adventures, experienced without fatigue or risk.

The next day I would resume my duties as a good girl. I served tea and petits fours to Amina's lady friends, half listened, or rather didn't listen at all, to the never-ending chatter, and continued to daydream while looking alert. I was terribly bored and wondered how long I would continue to live this life of waiting, how many years I would remain in this hybrid state of a young married girl, what miracle would get me out of this rut, where I was stuck with no benefit to anyone.

The miracle happened about a year after I arrived in Paris, in the simplest, most logical way in the world: the absolute ruin of my family, this time with no way back. The last pearl in the necklace had, as it were, been eaten. Without delay we had to dismiss the two servants and my brother's tutor, get rid of the fine apartment in the fine district and set to work. The most unrealistic of all these unpleasant economic imperatives was compulsory work for everyone, as it goes without saying that none of us had a job; worse still, we could do nothing with our hands or our brains.

Providence, which as one knows often comes up with good ideas at just the right time, provided solutions, shaky perhaps, but solutions nonetheless.

A friend of my parents', a former aristocrat too but rescued by a tremendously advantageous marriage, lent them a small apartment and a small sum that would bail them out for a time. My brother was sent to boarding school. As for me, Providence intervened again, suggesting an idea to my stepmother. An ingenious idea—the job for which I could perhaps apply required neither intelligence nor skill of any sort, simply a pleasant physique. Good Lord, no, not what some readers might imagine! We are talking about a job as a mannequin, a job that dozens of female émigrés were already doing, some of them real princesses. There would, therefore, be no disgrace in becoming a mannequin, quite possibly the reverse—the job had a certain prestige, as not everyone could do it. Better still, Amina had another idea that would boost my chances: she recommended me to the Worth couturiers, where she was a long-standing client.

Moreover—another piece of luck—I moved into a fine building on the Champ de Mars where another (still rich) female friend of my parents' lived. One detail did change the picture, though: I wasn't to live in the fine apartment, but would be lent a maid's room, temporarily vacant. I was jubilant.

Great Independence

I was free for the first time in my life, totally free, and it turned my head completely. There was an antidote to this intoxication that might have made me stone-cold sober: poverty and all its uncertainties. But not a bit of it. Improbable though it may seem to those who measure happiness in possessions, I was jubilant about poverty too. Destitution awoke an instinct that I'd always had deep within me and that sat alongside a violent appetite for life, a contradiction I can note but not explain. As a child in a world of multimillionaires, I had dreamt of poverty; was it a reaction to the pressure that money exerted on them? They talked only of inheritances past or future, argued bitterly about lawsuits that never ended and suspected each other of bad intentions. *Pul,* 'money' in our native tongue, was the word I heard most often as a child. It commanded fratricidal wars, fortunately only verbal, and consumed all the energy of the combatants.

Is this why I dreamt of poverty, but lived in dignity and order? I dreamt of living in a garret—a dream I haven't invented after the fact for literary effect. It obsessed me in my childhood, as I've written elsewhere. And now it had come true: I had my garret, a real old-fashioned one with a porthole window and without heating or running water. It was nothing like a domestic help's room in a modern building with central heating, water galore and a shower. In passing, let us salute progress or the trade unions who encouraged the 'reactionary forces' not to leave their servants shivering on the seventh floor while their own rooms were warm as toast.

My tiny garret had an iron bedstead, a table and chair in white wood and an uncertain piece of furniture that could at a pinch be called a dressing table, where I placed a bowl and jug. Wall hooks covered by a sheet constituted the wardrobe. A burner and a kerosene stove completed the furnishings with a monastic austerity, a quality I expected to rule out of my future lifestyle, which, I hoped, would be brilliant and perhaps dissolute.

Heart pounding and legs shaking, I presented myself at Worth on Rue de la Paix. I knew that my ample hips might pose an obstacle to my desired career in an arena that preferred the wooden plank-woman. Shamsi, who teased me so cruelly about my poorly placed curves, was convinced I would be sent packing 'with a whip'. He liked to paraphrase the historic quote ascribed to the Russian envoys sent to Prince Rurik of Scandinavia: 'Our land is great and abundant but there is no order in it. Come to reign and rule over us.' Shamsi maintained I had said to my husband, 'My buttocks are abundant, but have no order. Come to reign and rule over them.'

I would force a laugh when he trotted out this crude joke for the umpteenth time, then go and roll in secret on the floor in order to firm up my hips as some omniscient beautician had recommended.

When I was miraculously accepted by the recruiter, it was my turn to gloat. Granted, I trembled when her beady eyes fixed on the troublesome part of my figure, but she said nothing too severe. The *patron* himself came to oversee my application and approved it, but without enthusiasm, or so it seemed to me. What did it matter? I was to start on the first of the month, which was only a few days away. No one can imagine my joy, perhaps the greatest of my life; I was free and a mannequin, a combination that was more than I could have hoped for.

As I looked forward to this imminent day that was to mark my entry into the most stylish aspect of Parisian life and (I hoped) the most depraved, I moved into my humble abode, which hopelessly lacked sophistication.

The greatest drawback of my seventh-floor perch was the supposed lift. It was what they called a service lift and resembled a prison with its sinister black cage and the slow, gloomy passage of time inside, especially for me, as I'm claustrophobic. I don't know if the motor was bad-tempered, defective or just old, but it ascended with difficulty, producing an unpleasant clunk at every floor. The further up it went, the slower it got and the greater my anxiety. It sounded like a sick animal that was breathing its last. And one day the inevitable happened: having reached the sixth floor, the beast began to fall. Fortunately, it did not expend any force even in this descent, and arrived at the ground floor even more drained and weary than ever. That was the end of our relationship. I broke it off that day and walked up the seven flights of stairs, actually reaching my perch faster that way. I was getting hot and out of breath by the fifth floor, when a postcard image of Mont Blanc rose before me. This reflex was surprisingly frequent; I would see the snowy peaks of mountains and be gripped by nostalgia, a reference perhaps to Mount Kazbek, the highest summit in the Caucasus. Then it would all disappear and I would find myself gasping for breath on the service stairs of a Parisian building.

Despite the extreme modesty of my new abode, I was already living in the most beautiful castles of Spain and my ambitions blossomed in the shade of their colonnades, with no regard for reality or practicality. Resolved to 'live my life', I saw it would be glittering and strewn with the corpses of heartbroken admirers. It was obvious to me that a life worth living had to dazzle. I just didn't know how it would do this. But the job of mannequin seemed an excellent springboard to launch me up and away. I would be queen of Paris, and while awaiting my coronation would go and work—a prospect that alarmed me, as I was extremely shy. I've hardly mentioned it until now, but in my youth it was a real handicap.

The fateful morning arrived. I gulped down a café crème in a bistro and reported to Worth on the Rue de la Paix at nine o'clock sharp.

When I look back over my already very long life, I am always surprised, astounded even, by its not terribly poetic resemblance to a Neapolitan ice cream with its layers of different colours and flavours. Perhaps every life can be seen in this way, more or less. Mine has a particularly large number of layers, so dissimilar, so different in inspiration, that it's hard to imagine one and the same destiny behind them.

I find it hard to believe that in some mysterious way the little Caucasian goose was my ancestor, and I am annoyed rather than touched by the thought. That morning, this Caucasian goose took on an unthinkable role. Her grandmother and even her mother had been veiled and legal minors all their lives, subservient first to their fathers then to their husbands, who could have divorced them on a whim. How could that grandmother, or mother, have imagined me parading dresses, some very low-cut, in front of strangers, as they had never heard of such a thing?

But reality prevailed: the goose from the Caucasus was going to disguise herself as a model at one of the most prestigious fashion houses in Paris, even the world, with all the risks this role entailed.

So began my Haute Couture era-layer, of which I have tangible souvenirs in the form of photos taken for fashion magazines.

*

A small, desiccated person inspected me so disdainfully that I thought my first hour at the fashion house was going to be my last. I was wrong. Madame Blanche might have the right to look down on me, but she couldn't sack me. Like an apostle, only the *patron* could unbind what he had bound, and even if the aforesaid Blanche had wanted to dispatch me to hell so that my expansive hips and child's shoulders might perish in the flames, she couldn't. Icily silent, she led me to a workshop where a virago with a moustache dripping in sweat took my measurements amid further scorn: they cast me into that section of humanity whose proportions did not correspond to the laws of haute couture. Next, Madame Blanche led me to what was known as the 'mannequins' cabin': who had given this name (and how and why), redolent of liners sailing on the high seas, to the den where the young ladies were held between displaying the collections? I will never know: another curiosity destined to remain unsatisfied.

I found around twenty girls there, each taller and more beautiful than the last and wearing the same uniform: a straight-cut dress the colour of lilac, decorated with a little collar and cuffs in white stitching which made the brightest of them look like schoolgirls. When I saw them, I understood Madame Blanche's scorn towards me: my average height, my hips—the only glorious part of my person—my oriental face, my lack of elegance were all shocking among these giants with slender thighs, pink complexions and the bearing of Diana the Huntress. I cursed destiny for not making Batignolles my birthplace. 'Little darkie,' said a blonde queen as she looked at me, without ill will it should be said, and from that point on I was the 'little darkie' to everyone. The next day, when I too donned the lilac uniform, which had been whipped up in no time, I blended in slightly more with my colleagues. True, it was better not to examine me too closely, but taken as a whole and viewed from a distance I could pass for one of the crowd.

I was shown into the spacious pen lined with identical dressing tables, one for each mannequin, and was assigned mine. I sat and looked without pleasure at the 'little darkie' reflected in the mirror. How I disliked her, how tired I was of meeting her, or rather of dragging her around, always the same no matter where I took her.

I was surprised to hear a familiar language interrupting these depressing thoughts: Russian. I turned and saw two girls, one with fiery red hair, white skin and an aggressive manner, the other with a cat's face, wide eyes and a small pink nose; both beautiful, both common. They spoke loudly, dismissive of those around them, their attitude typical of many émigrés who tended to treat France as a hostile country, holding it somehow responsible for their misfortune, criticizing everything, dissatisfied with everything, crying at every opportunity: 'Oh, at home…', 'U nas…'

Hélène and Sandra lived like Siamese twins, not out of affection or for mutual support in a foreign land, but in order to quarrel about everything, which is after all another form of solidarity. Their way of speaking, their gestures and behaviour, revealed their lowly origins, though both claimed to be of aristocratic stock, if not nieces of the tsar's. The French girls alongside them in the shared cabin rarely if ever came from what is known as 'good society', so could not spot the indicators of social standing, and were so proud to be neighbours of these noble foreigners that they forgave them their impenetrable language and wounding particularism.

As soon as Hélène and Sandra learnt of my Caucasian origins, they tried to 'colonize' me, but I didn't respond, firstly because I had no fondness for their manner. I was more curious about the 'natives', who to me embodied a reverse exoticism that I wanted to know, feel, understand. Secondly, I was exasperated, as I always am, by Russians' efforts to assimilate me; this form of imperialism even among émigrés awoke in me all the reflexive responses of colonized peoples, since that is what my people had been and still are. Me, Russian? Why not Papuan? Yes, I was born in a Russian colony; yes, I'm a former subject of the tsar's, but I'm not Russian in my heart or religion or ethnic origin. I did not hate the colonizers as my fiercely Muslim grandmothers had done, but I kept my distance and did not want to be 'one of them'. But that's enough on this subject—I might return to it later.

So I spurned the advances of Hélène and Sandra, and allied myself with a girl who had such an extraordinary number of beauty spots that I compared her face to a starry sky. And her first name, Albertine, delighted me: not because of Proust, whom I had never heard of at that time, but because of its sweet melody. Albertine herself was sweet too, and good-natured and a great help in my apprenticeship in this new life.

First of all, she taught me an essential art: that of walking in the salons with the air of a haughty, distant princess, made more difficult on the one hand by our intense curiosity about the clients, whom we envied with all our might, and on the other by the need to avoid treading on their carelessly outstretched feet. We would pass very close to them, while appearing to ignore their presence, our manner clearly showing that we just happened to be walking there for our own diversion; the clients were present simply to adorn our way.

Albertine taught me the art of removing make-up without water, of using saliva on mascara, of polishing my nails on the skin of my thighs, of putting on dresses with maximum speed and minimum damage, of applying make-up subtly, that is to say, of squeezing from one's face, like a lemon, all the goodness it can provide. Such an enlightened intelligence concerning the requirements of our professional life filled me with respect. In all other areas of her life, however, Albertine seemed more helpless than a child: she could barely read, didn't know how to cook an egg, was incapable of formulating an idea, and spent her time away from Parisian haute couture eating, sleeping, titivating and making love. Since she lived in a hotel, she would say with notice-able satisfaction that she 'didn't lift a finger around the house'.

'You see,' she explained to me, our mutual liking encouraging confidences, 'my friend doesn't want me to get tired after work. I wouldn't be any good at making love. Do you see now?'

Oh yes, I saw very well! Her next remark made the relation-ship even clearer.

'That's why he wants me to live in the hotel, so I don't have to do anything: no housework or shopping or cooking. He pays and I...'

An imperious wave of the hand implied her generosity of spirit in consenting to this arrangement. Moreover, I saw the undeniable logic in her friend's point of view and envied Albertine, to whom destiny had given such a prudent guide.

Like all simple people she had a limited vocabulary and showed an inopportune predilection for the word 'so', which she scattered liberally into her conversation. Her essential charm came from her candour, similar to a sheep's, which her friend must have greatly appreciated, judging from the sums he lavished on this angelic and so attractively empty head.

I paid her a visit one day, and had to admit that her living arrangements had great advantages. She rented a room with a bathroom, an amenity she was justifiably proud of, in a *semi-luxe* hotel. She ordered tea and pastries by telephone, explaining to me that she always had her meals sent up to her room, as she was too lazy to go down to the bar and restaurant, and her friend feared encounters that might pose a danger to her virtue. Clearly in these circumstances it would be superfluous 'to lift a finger', and I confess that I felt a pinch of envy when I compared her luxury to my garret without heating or running water and with seven interminable flights of stairs to get there.

Her masseur came while I was still there. Albertine got undressed in a trice, her professional skills in evidence, lay down on her back, and the man began to knead her flesh, puffing like a grampus. I was suddenly overwhelmed by memories, not so distant after all, of another, very different, massage: my enormous grandmother, with layers of belly and thighs the size of fortress towers, lying on her bed, calling us to a special event—by 'us', I mean half a dozen of her grandsons and granddaughters aged between six and twelve. We would take off our shoes, if we weren't already barefoot, as this usually happened in the countryside, jump onto the bed and from there onto the mass of flesh, which would already be groaning in anticipation of pleasure and pain—and we would stamp on her with fury, using all our strength, shouting and ululating, giving ourselves up to a sort of wild dance where we released, as they say today, hidden impulses. And while we yelled, Grandmother would let out long moans, interspersed with cries of 'Ay Allah' when the pleasure of the flesh became nothing but pain.

These two massages—these two worlds, past and present—mixed in my mind, especially when Albertine began to moan in pain too. But there was a cruel difference between her prettily proportioned body, unmarred by any fat at all, and that of the old woman, doomed to oriental immobility, and I tried to dismiss the image of a deformed mass. Would I be like her one day thanks to some law of heredity that I could not escape?

Despite all the interest Albertine took in me, she could not bring herself to compliment me on my figure, which she must have found unattractive. But, generous soul that she was, she took the trouble to try to improve me, even going so far as to give me her own box of mascara, stuck into a compact lump by her saliva. Maybe she saw this box as a kind of magic gift, destined to transform me into a Parisienne. Through sheer determination Albertine succeeded in making me look ten years older, getting rid of my overly 'natural' appearance, which was astonishing in

Paris, and even more so in a fashion house where everything was artifice and refinement. She took an equal interest in my social situation, disapproving of my lack of a man, young or old. In her mind my chastity was a flaw that needed urgent correction, and she was ready to work on it.

'So, you've no idea. Then what? So, you're going to stay high and dry? I'll ask my friend to find you someone. He meets lots of people at the Bourse.'

I begged her not to do anything, and she gave in easily. She had made the suggestion out of kind-heartedness, after all. She must have secretly thought that I was impossible to 'marry off', though to her, 'married off' meant 'kept', nothing more. Now, as everyone, or rather every woman, knows only too well, kept women stroll upon this earth in excessive numbers, while 'serious friends' are hard to find. Even if I'd been beautiful, this search would have run into an unexpected obstacle: I still had archaic ideas about love, and the idea of making it a source of material gain horrified me. I was attracted only by reciprocal, disinterested feelings, I told Albertine, who became indignant at such heresy. How could I get this so wrong? According to her, God had created man with the sole purpose of making him spend as much money as he could and more on woman. He had to cough up, the rest was just a distraction. And when he showed a regrettable tendency not to put his hand in his pocket, he should not be encouraged; on the contrary, he should be reminded of his obligations always and everywhere, and if necessary be forced to meet them.

'So, do you understand? Are you mad? You will ruin the profession, behaving like that. So, if nice little women like you make love for free, then what? Where do we go?' she asked me, irritated despite her good nature, the first time we touched on the inexhaustible and fascinating subject of our relations with the enemy sex.

'Men are selfish,' she resumed, her irritation having quickly passed, 'so if you don't ask them for anything, they'll be only too happy. They'll make love, and that's the last you'll see of them. So no, that would be too easy.'

The need to show the collection interrupted this perceptive exploration of male psychology, but we resumed it later, and the next day, and it became our main, if not only, topic of discussion. Albertine could not bear my confused ideas. Besides, men, money and 'love', or rather all three bound fast in a closed circuit, constituted the psychological nourishment of these attractive young women locked in their cabin. Their conversation would often degenerate into impassioned debate and require a call to order from Madame Blanche, the duenna, the keeper responsible for the good behaviour of this cackling hen coop. Twenty healthy young women, ill-mannered and not given to introspection, can make a lot of noise.

The mannequins who had a 'serious, wealthy friend' enjoyed a well-deserved prestige and rested on their often hard-won laurels. Those who were badly 'married', or not married at all, secretly envied them, making every effort on the sly to assess the value of the happy elect's clothes and jewels and complaining openly of their own bad luck. They all had the same goal, though: marriage, with town hall, wedding ring, church and fortune, the crowning of their career, the pinnacle of earthly bliss. Even the most shameless harboured a fondness for bourgeois respectability and none of the glory of being a 'kept' woman could extinguish that longing, anchored in the depths of their being and rooted in centuries of tradition, no doubt. We were still a long way from the permissive society and women's lib.

Their psychological emptiness and their lack of culture and curiosity did not bother them in the least—they weren't even aware of it. Read? Out of the question. Their intelligence was untouched by the famous mass media, as it did not yet exist. When they did happen to venture into topics beyond the men-love-money trinity, they would spout nonsense. The very beautiful Lucette, thin as a liana, tall, and unreal as a ray of moonlight, declared to me one day, in order to crush the foreigner with the grandeur of France, that the 'magnificent' Grand Palais had been built by Louis XIV to house his mistresses. No one contradicted her. They listened to her with respect.

Did this poverty, both intellectual and artistic, bother me? I was often asked this question later. No, because I was here only to earn my crust and I had opportunities elsewhere, especially at the Josézous's, to educate myself and move in other worlds.

After just one year in Paris I had not yet forgotten the misery of a country in revolution, and was enchanted by the luxury of the Worth fashion house. I appreciated the elegance of the dresses, the opulence of the furs, the generous light and heat in the salons, where everything shone all day long: the chandeliers, the mirrors, the silk dresses, the young girls' complexions. Yes, I marvelled at all this, as thanks to my supposedly barbaric origins I had and still have a love of brilliance: the more brightly things shine, the happier I am.

I joined Worth when they were preparing their winter collection, so like the others I had to stand sometimes for half a day, waiting for the inspiration of the designers, which could be slow in coming. The *patron* also designed for the collection, of course, but he worked with only two models—the most beautiful of all, with a hieratic deportment, who inspired him to design evening wear of Byzantine magnificence. The other girls went to his creative studio only to accompany the senior designers from the twenty-four ateliers, when they had to show him their designs in development. Sometimes we had to wait our turn in a corner, immobile, bored stiff, while the *patron* of *patrons* criticized, adjusted, gave his approval or pronounced his veto.

Once the novelty had worn off, the 'cabin' began to weigh on me, not morally, but physically. The mannequins and dressers lived in a haze of perfume, which made me dizzy and gave me migraines, and of gossip, which was always the same. There were too many people in this limited space, too many voices, too many faces, too much monotony, broken only by the alarming bustle of the shows. Then, everything flew: shouts, hair, dresses, calls for help, insults, orders; the dressers didn't know where to turn first and a cloud of rice powder hung above it all, pierced by the icy gaze of Madame Blanche.

*

After six months, the *patron* had me dismissed by that same Madame Blanche, who took visible pleasure in carrying out this order. I suspected that the *patron* had only kept me on so long out of regard for Amina; my middling height compared to the other models and my lack of elegance and Parisian chic got the better of his courtesy. For the sake of my self-esteem, I'll leave it at that.

He gave me a month's wages and the lilac dress, and I left the Rue de la Paix on a fine spring day, not without pleasure. I couldn't bear the overcrowded, overheated, overexcited cabin any longer and I had no regrets at leaving kind-hearted Albertine who, discouraged by my stubborn virtue, had abandoned me to my fate as a disinterested woman.

'So, when you're married…' she said to me in farewell, pursing her lips to convey her doubts about my future.

I left with eight hundred francs in my pocket and plenty of optimism. While Islam was no longer an active presence in my life, I remained attached to it by an umbilical cord: fatalism. One cannot praise highly enough this psychological disposition that suppresses revolt in situations where it would be pointless. Unfortunately, if in the past Islam abused fatalism, it seems to be cured of it today.

Allah rewarded me very quickly for my submission to his decrees: he directed my steps along the path of chance to the Place Vendôme, where the luxury shops insulted the poor with their sumptuous displays. I allowed myself the luxury of dreaming at the sight of jewels resting on their bed of velvet, and in particular of a diadem of diamonds that I would buy at once to wear to the ball at the Opéra that same evening. The purchase made, I continued on my way, and a few buildings further on saw a notice posted at the entrance to a fashion house: they were looking for a model, size 42. I overcame my shyness and walked up the service stairs. The concerns of conscious and organized capitalism did not permit me to use the 'luxury' staircase. The stairs weren't even lit, and I groped my way up to a room cluttered with boxes, clothes and tissue paper—it was the packing room. I was led, more dead than alive, to the *patron*, who looked me up and down with a piercing eye, and finding me to his liking as a couturier engaged me on the spot, without even making me put on a garment to display. I was flabbergasted. I still remember this immediate good fortune as one of the rare successes of my life, achieved without the slightest effort, when success usually required long, arduous efforts made in anxiety and fear of failure. I am well acquainted with the torture of hope.

*

This house of modest dimensions but worldwide renown specialized in tailoring, and at that time dressed the smartest ladies in France, the two Americas and England. The three models, four including me, all of middling height—not the 'beautiful willows' in vogue at Worth—cultivated the 'young girl' look sought by the *patron*, so I found myself in a world of my own proportions and felt comfortable in this new cabin, where there were only four of us plus one dresser. But the atmosphere and conversations were identical to those I already knew by heart: the obsession with the circle money-gentleman friend, love-money, gentleman friend-money, and then money-money, love-love, gentleman friend-gentleman friend... But since this obsession gripped only four people instead of twenty-four, it was considerably alleviated.

At the risk of becoming repetitive, I must return once more to the singular psychology of the models, who in some respects had something of the prostitute about them; but no, that's going too far, it would be more accurate to say something of the courtesan. I am talking about the past, since I imagine that things have changed greatly in fifty years, thanks to mass media. They are rightly criticized, but, things being what they are (i.e. deeply ambiguous), they have their good points too: the media can open minds to multiple horizons. In my day my fellow models tended towards infantilism, pursuing only one goal, money, which they endeavoured to acquire by the surrender, lengthy or otherwise, of their charms, charms that with impeccable logic they would spend days on end perfecting. They seemed unaware that the insatiable beast that is man sometimes looks for qualities other than the physical. It didn't occur to them that another part of ourselves, perhaps the most precious, also requires as much care and ornament as our external appearance, if not more.

When the day came that their serious friend left them, they never looked for the cause in their abandonment of themselves, but in the ignominy of the male, and the tone and substance of their grievances did not change. This is how they would usually begin: 'Getting a man isn't everything. You have to know how to keep him.'

'Oh yes!' the chorus of abused and disillusioned women would sigh.

'All men are bastards,' delivered with the bitterness of a thousand years of experience, would round off the complaints about the congenital cruelty of men. This enemy, this cruel maniac, this animal should be bled dry as long as he desired you. The monster had to be fought ceaselessly or he would devour you.

This attitude was based on evidence that the most second-rate intelligence could not fail to notice: liaisons lasted only as long as desire. Aware of this, without wanting or being able to discern the reason, the mannequins did their best to exploit the situation thoroughly for as long as it lasted. It goes without saying that friendship and trust were ruled out of these relationships dominated by rapaciousness.

*

The influence of the milieu, the 'culture' that we set such store by today, put an end to the idealism of my adolescence in which Lenin held a special place. Instead of singing the virtues of socialism, my mind focused on acquiring a cross-fox fur, a crocodile handbag or, more boldly, that symbol of success—a mink coat. The fact that I did not wear such a thing until some thirty years later, and then made from pieces, not whole pelts, is proof of my failure to succeed.

The comedy and the tragedy of this story is that the desire for material goods can torment you just as much as other, more noble, desires, and the job of mannequin seems to me especially unhealthy, because the temptation of luxury is everywhere, and luxury is impossible to attain through your own resources, i.e. the meagre wages at the end of the month. We lived in an atmosphere of refinement that impressed on us a taste for beautiful clothes, bags, shoes and hats that we couldn't afford, so we stewed in a sense of frustration and envy, if not outright revolt. Our troubles, though not so respectable, were nonetheless real, even if a philosopher would find them contemptible. I've always thought that the intensity of our sorrows is not measured by their cause, be it dramatic or trivial; that's why the sorrow of a child whose toy has been taken away can be as intense as any other pain.

I speak as one who knows the torment that a cross fox artfully displayed in a shop window can cause. I sacrificed plenty of lunches in order to buy one of those dead animals with its pointed snout and glassy look, and I confess to having rarely felt a purer happiness than on the day when I was finally able, at the expense of my stomach, to place one on my shoulders. In an excess of stupidity, in those distant days we wore them casually thrown over our shoulders, depriving them of their sole practical purpose, that of keeping us warm. When after long months of covetousness I finally possessed this decorative fur, it had already become commonplace and unfashionable. And in turn, fashion, obsessively capricious, would produce something else to tempt us. So one was never satisfied, always prey to desire. Perhaps that is the very essence of the human condition.

So why the surprise that girls were no longer 'honest'? Some would have sold not only themselves, but their father and mother as well, in exchange for riches, so heavily did temptation weigh.

*

Hollywood stars, the wives of great industrialists and politicians, and exotic beauties came to lord it over us at our fine salons at the Place Vendôme. They flaunted their opulence, making us horribly jealous. The more beautiful, famous and visibly adored by their male companion they were, the more we hated them. This unhealthy job as a model infected me with an odious sense of envy, ensnared as I was by the lure of sordid materialism in all its finery. For the first time in my life, I lost interest in reading, which had never happened since I learnt the alphabet, so deeply had the contagion that is frivolousness eaten away at me. My 'lux-omania' took grotesque forms: for example, I imagined myself dripping in jewels and honours in the grandstand as my race-horse finished first, bringing me a surfeit of fame and fortune; or, richly dressed (of course), and as always dripping in jewels, I was in a columned hall, receiving Parisian high society, who were all flattered to be there. I dreamt of luxury cabins, luxury cars, luxury lovers, luxury horses. *Non-luxe* was strictly banished from my deluxe life, though the evil of *non-luxe* pounced on me when I climbed my service stairs puffing like a grampus.

It was in one of the fine salons where we showed the garments that I suffered one of the greatest disappointments of my youth. As a child I had been passionately in love with Francesca Bertini, a celebrated star of the cinema whom I thought sublimely beautiful, divinely elegant, epithets that I considered inadequate at the time of my infatuation. Thanks to her films, which came to Baku in rapid succession, I knew all my idol's outfits down to the last detail, oddly the same in several films—today, we cannot imagine a star or starlet wearing the same dress in two consecutive films.

I knew all her expressions, as monotonous as her outfits; I noted her every pose and gesture. I would imitate her when I was at last alone in my room; I would proudly throw my head back like her; I would wring my hands like her; like her, I would cast killer looks at objects that stood in for admirers and died by the dozen of love for me, alias Francesca Bertini. In a nutshell, I adored her but didn't envy her; there was no resentment or grinding of teeth about my genuine admiration.

Now, some ten or twelve years later in Paris, when we were rehearsing the showing of the collection, a sales assistant came to tell us that an Italian star was in the salon. When she said her name, my blood froze: the inimitable Francesca Bertini was there, and I was going to see her.

I recognized her immediately, though real life had warped my dreams. Not only did I see her, I touched her too; she liked the coat that I was showing and wanted to try it. I took it off and helped her put it on. How can I convey the violence of my disappointment? If someone did the impossible and proved to me the mediocrity of Bach, my bitterness could not be any greater. Tall and slender on screen, in reality Francesca Bertini seemed short and ordinary, without grace or brilliance, barely elegant.

Good God, I thought in dismay, this is 'my' Francesca Bertini, the object of all those hours of daydreaming when I should have been asleep!

Meanwhile, she was haggling with the saleswoman as though she were at Les Halles, oblivious to the drama I was experiencing.

We were living through the liveliest, most prosperous years after the war, the *Années folles* that I've already mentioned. The car was already devouring Paris; the hotels were packed with American tourists for whom the Russian émigrés provided numerous night clubs, one of their specialities. Dance floors shook under the assault of the foxtrotters; the flappers, without knowing it the grandmothers of women's lib, flapped furiously. A thousand and one things gave the city a festive atmosphere, which one hoped would be permanent after the horrible massacres of the war so recently ended—and, one thought, ended for good.

While the salons were empty, we would often settle comfortably at the windows and watch with malicious glee the hundreds of cars jammed into the Place Vendôme, perhaps doomed never to move again. In summer, hot air rose up to us, polluted with petrol fumes from all those steel lungs trapped at our feet. But if I looked up, I could see Napoleon perched on his column, aloof from the mechanical life that had come to a halt below; did he dream he was on top of a pyramid and flying over the centuries? I brought him down to integrate him into ours; I sat him in a huge limousine, had him disembark from a gigantic aeroplane. I converted him into 'little General Bonaparte' who

went to have tea with Joséphine opposite the Ritz or to cash a
cheque at the Westminster Bank next door to us.

The awful racket of hundreds of horns would interrupt my
historical game and we would leave our observation point, closing the windows on the noise and heat of the asphalted city, on
the foul air saturated with petrol, and return to our conversations
on the trinity—gentlemen friends, love, money.

During the worst heat of August, when the elect of this world
ate their fill of ice cream, fanning themselves with cool air, we
were putting on big, supposedly comfortable, coats and, worse
still, furs, as we were already preparing or, rather, showing the
winter collection. We felt our bones liquefy beneath the furs;
our feet turned into large swollen objects, burnt by the polish of
the shoes and the thick carpets that we walked across. Powder
became paste, mascara ran; our hatred for the customers collapsed on sofas and armchairs was never greater. Did they ever
put themselves in our place? I doubt it. Humour deserted us.
We didn't even have the strength to smile when an American
woman asked to see a tailored 'streetwalker suit', rather than a
'walking suit', or when the *patron*, who fancied himself a wit,
came up with some supposed bon mot that only he found funny.

I have yet to introduce the 'monkey', as we called him among
ourselves, conforming to an old, if not ancient, tradition. A small,
lean man with a great, curved beak for a nose and a military
air, he would adopt a strict tone with us, his slaves, which was
just for show. He even affected roughness with the customers,
while flattering them at the same time; a combination that he
used with perfect poise, pleasing both himself and the buyers.

While we were parading in the salon, dressed in beautiful
clothes but inhabited by ugly thoughts, the 'monkey' would

position himself at the door to the salon, casting his penetrating gaze all around and barking an order from time to time in the tone of a sergeant major. Despite his rustic manners, he had a keen sense of elegance and his designs were the height of good taste. So the reputation of his fashion house crossed mountains, seas and oceans, bringing him a vast clientele and considerable fortune. A small tailor from the Basque country, he had become a world-renowned couturier.

*

As I've said, there were three other models in the cabin, whom I should introduce to you: blonde Yvette, slim both physically and morally and with fine but sharp facial features. Paradoxically, given the environment, she was a redoubtable petite bourgeoise committed to the proprieties. We nicknamed her 'the lady'. Though we considered it laughable, the name suited her.

'Yes,' she would say, 'I'm the only lady among the lot of you,' and would resume sorting the lingerie with an ironic pout in our direction. She was mistaken in considering herself a lady, but less so in denying us that appellation.

Mary, Marie in civilian life, had all the trappings of the 'non-lady': her accent, her behaviour, the extreme freedom of her language placed her firmly in that social category. Her erotic exploits were far more daring than any my shy imagination could invent. Pretty, jolly, witty, she was also, remarkably, extremely intelligent.

My third colleague, Lucie, was radiantly blonde and stupid as a goose, but very kind. In this milieu, foolishness was common currency, but Lucie's did not cease to amaze the most hardened of us. To get the simplest notion into her head, we had to repeat it to her many times, otherwise she would get the wrong end of the stick. Despite or because of her intellectual innocence, Lucie had the protection of a 'very serious' friend, so serious that he kept her like a princess, luring her with the prospect of imminent marriage, which she looked forward to calmly and hopefully. Remembering Albertine, I wondered if a certain type of innocent stupidity attracts men, in particular rich ones. Lucie, with her simple soul, did not boast about her good fortune—which was just as well for her! For a girl so foolish to be so lucky could be borne only if she was humble at the same time. We bullied her quite often to avenge the envy we felt, but she put up with it without resentment.

I spent five and a half days out of seven with these girls and the dresser. Always the first to arrive, I would begin with a lengthy, painstaking job that required all my concentration: putting on my make-up. Then I would polish my nails or remove hair. Whereupon the others would arrive: placid Lucie, the 'lady' wrapped in haughty airs, lips pursed, and last of all Mary, noisy, dishevelled, none too clean, but pretty with her messy hair, with its silken sheen, and her beautiful, greedy mouth. She would begin by complaining, 'Oh, what a bitch of a life. I didn't get a wink of sleep. You know the type…'

An account of a night of tumultuous love would follow, only to be interrupted by a saleswoman at the door of the cabin calling, 'Come along, girls, the collection…'

'Dirty whores,' Mary would grumble, meaning the clients. 'It's obvious they can sleep all night. They don't have to bust a gut for a man.'

We would begin by putting on the designs with as much apathy as distaste, but our ill will would cease as soon as the 'monkey' arrived to shake us up. Then we would become swift and light. We would glide from salon to salon, instead of dragging our feet one after the other in front of the hated clients. We would pass through again when the clients were numerous, their number in part justifying our efforts. But when we had to show two or three of these ogresses, sometimes just one, the sixty to eighty pieces in the collection, we would suffocate with rage. We could see social inequity in all its cruelty—which mattered to us only when we had it on our backs (literally)—and would curse the privileges of the rich, appealing to divine justice and, since this was too often absent, to world revolution. This was the time to remember my flirtation with Lenin.

At midday, having shown the collection several times in succession, we would have lunch in one of the cheap but excellent cafes or restaurants that proliferated in the Place Vendôme area at that time. Then we would go and walk in the Tuileries or do some shopping in the large shops nearby until two, when we would return to work. At six we were free again. The young ladies met their gentlemen friends, some more serious than others, while I was unemployed, alone with my liberty, which I had so aspired to. Independence finally acquired sat in my hands like a wonderful fruit, from which I didn't know how to extract the juice. The idea of taking a lover terrified me as though it were a step of incalculable consequence. Not in terms of virtue, and even less so from a fear of sin, a Christian idea that did not bother me in the least since I was unaware of it: rather, I had a sort of fear of men, of physical intimacy in which I had done a wretched apprenticeship with an unloved husband. I lived on the idealized memory of Andrei Massarin, the Prince Charming of my adolescence, who had satisfied my most absurd dreams without imposing on me the brutality of physical love. Where would I find another like him? I looked for him in every man I met, and of course I found no more than a caricature. Was I aware of how much my mind had confused him with Andrei Bolkonsky from *War and Peace*? From the outset I had thought him his very incarnation. I had endowed him with everything that a very young and madly fanciful mind could see as desirable in a hero. In other words, the need for the absolute was already spoiling for me people of flesh and blood who lived in the everyday—and, moreover, the whole of existence in general, thus condemning me to depressing dissatisfaction. Sometimes a whole life is not enough to cure a mind of the sickness of excessive imagination.

While waiting for the Great Hero of my dreams, I fell in love with Napoleon and Louis XIV in turn, who at least had the advantage of expanding my scant cultural knowledge through the books I read about them, and sparing me the suffering of real love.

Time passed in this way. Luckily I had the Josézous, whose warmth revived me, but life seemed monotonous again—until one day the extraordinary occurred.

A Tale of the Unexpected

The monotony of my life ended one Saturday afternoon, when the Josézous and I were quietly digesting our frugal lunch—frugal for fear of putting on weight. Zuleykha was painting a lampshade across which knights chased each other brandishing lances; José was playing a game of patience, which my father had taught him, with me overseeing operations, when suddenly—and this 'when suddenly' isn't a literary device but literal accuracy—when suddenly we heard hurried steps in the courtyard, which made us prick up our ears. Then the door, which was never locked, crashed open without so much as a knock and a voice I would have recognized in a crowd of thousands cried, 'Are you here?'

'Gulnar?' I cried in turn, dashing towards my onrushing cousin. 'It's you, it's really you…' is all I managed to say.

'Yes, it's me, of course it's me, it's me, it's me.'

We covered each other in kisses, laughing, crying, babbling incoherently.

Then she tore herself out of my arms and launched herself on Zuleykha and the whole reunion process was repeated. Finally, having had her fill of cousinly kisses, Gulnar looked at José, who had naturally got to his feet to follow events more closely.

'Is this the husband?' she asked in French, and without dropping a beat added in Azeri, 'But he's ugly!'

We were so astonished—José isn't ugly at all—that we didn't have the wit to reply. Gulnar had flung herself on him anyway and was embracing him with charming but perhaps slightly over-the-top effusion. But I was wrong; Gulnar's inclination towards excess led me to twist her intentions.

Zuleykha asked her the crucial question: 'Where have you come from?'

'From Moscow, via Warsaw and Berlin. Don't I look chic?' She puffed herself up, the better to show off her grey suit, which was so well cut that even I, accustomed to the best Parisian couturiers, could find nothing to criticize.

'Have you remarried?' I asked, immediately realizing the stupidity of my question. She replied carelessly, 'A husband... I'll tell you all about it later. I've got so many stories to tell.'

I could easily believe it. She must have bucketloads of stories of every shape and colour, all with men as their common thread.

Then she took a bizarre object out of her bag, a magnificent lorgnette in engraved gold, and studied the studio from side to side and floor to ceiling. I watched her open-mouthed. Gulnar will never, ever cease to amaze me, I said to myself: the grandstanding arrival, the nonchalance, the lorgnette worthy of a dowager duchess from the Boulevard Saint-Germain or St Petersburg.

The examination complete, she closed the lorgnette with a swift flick of her hand and said condescendingly: 'Well really, there's no point being in Paris if you're going to live in a stable. And there's no denying this is a stable.'

She spoke French quickly and badly, and this ease even when making mistakes was Gulnar all over. I should add that after three months her French was flawless, because of the gift for languages and genius for adaptation she had always shown.

'You should know, my dearr, that you are in an artist's studio,' José interjected haughtily, suddenly recovering his wounded hidalgo pride. 'It was in a studio just like this one that El Greco and Michelangelo, Vermeer and Rubens painted.'

Gulnar was not to be intimidated by such details. Shrugging, she replied, 'I don't know them. I leave this studio and all those painters to you. At least you're charming, and you're the first painter I've ever met.'

'Instead of numbing our minds with this nonsense, tell us how you found out my address,' Zuleykha said, annoyed for the studio and for José.

'It was child's play. When I was in Berlin, I managed to get our president's telephone number' (she was referring to the ex-president of the ex-free and independent Azerbaijani Republic) 'and I called him when I got here. Voila.'

'You are clever,' I said. My lifelong admiration for her speed of mind and inventiveness was flooding back. Zuleykha's sharp intelligence seemed ponderous in comparison.

'You know perfectly well that I'm intelligent!'

'I can see you don't suffer from modesty,' José grumbled. His reason disapproved, yet his painter's eye very much approved. Not that Gulnar was especially beautiful, but she had that striking physique that captures the attention, and enthralled not so much with the features of her exotic face, pretty though they were, but with the mobility and unexpectedness of her expressions. She possessed to the highest degree that renowned, valuable charm that can be used to help or harm others. I suspected that, so far, she had used it only to gain advantage for herself.

In order to explain our relationship, I should take a leap into the past when Gulnar, her brothers and I were only children. They had been my teachers and I their disciple. My cousins had absorbed everything that a precocious mind could learn in childhood and passed it on to me, embellished with relevant commentaries and sometimes practical demonstrations. None of the bedtime stories that people read to children at that time, in the hope of keeping them innocent for as long as possible, could withstand their critical examination or their curiosity, which was always on the lookout for the unknowable. Their cynicism brought down the fragile edifice of beliefs that my German governess had sought to inculcate in me. Though she didn't trust them, she could never have imagined the effect of their teaching. In retrospect, I thanked the heavens for sparing her the horror she would have felt had she discovered the truth.

I admired them, and tried in vain to equal them in terms of cynicism, because I had neither their temperament nor audacity. Of my three small masters, I admired Gulnar in particular. Two years older than me chronologically, she was ten years older than me mentally. She knew everything, saw everything, guessed everything and explained it all to me. She was never at a loss for lies, inventions and schemes. Her temperament, which was already powerful at puberty, developed over the years to become incendiary, and while, like me, she married at the age of fifteen, it did her no harm at all, quite the reverse. She married a good, shy, ugly boy whom she cheated on enthusiastically, whom she left only to return to when it suited her, and whom she finally abandoned for good. Since leaving the Caucasus, I had heard nothing more from her or the other relatives who had remained over there, all communication between our two worlds having seemingly been cut off, partly because of practical problems: letters might arrive, and there again they might not. Moreover, under the new regime installed in the Caucasus, people were afraid of being compromised by sending letters abroad, which still applies today. Though I regretted not knowing what had happened to our close relatives—I wasn't a monster, after all—this rupture with a world where I had known so much sorrow was good for me. I felt liberated from it once and for all. I remember that, during my first years in France, when I had a nightmare it was always the same: I was back in Baku, stuck to the bottom of a black hole with the certainty that I would never escape weighing on me like a tombstone. I would struggle in vain against this suffocating load and would wake up, heart thumping in panic, but with immediate relief at finding myself in Paris, not at the bottom of a hole but in bed, bathed in the temperate climate of France, temperate in all respects.

'Where are you staying?' Zuleykha asked.

'At the Grand, of course.'

This 'of course' reminded me of the pre-war days, when the Caucasians would always stay at this hotel and nowhere else. Amina notably stayed there in 1913, with my eldest sister, of whom we had heard no news for years. These memories had certainly determined Gulnar's choice.

She didn't want to stay there, but wanted to find an apartment near the Josézous, furnished or not, as quickly as possible, straightaway if possible. She wanted to feel the warmth of family reunion. She wanted, desired, wished…

And chance, which so often favoured her, decreed that a furnished apartment should be free a few houses away, and that the owner of the building should be at home at that moment. The deal was concluded immediately, and the decision taken to move in the next day. I was to leave my maid's room and move in with Gulnar. While waiting for the next day's move, I was to spend the night in the hotel so that she did not feel abandoned there. We were not going to be separated again, she declared.

She decided, commanded, stunned us, charmed us, annoyed us, showed us plenty of proof that she controlled events rather than letting them control her. She beat her drum in her own way, indulging her fantasies, her endless fantasies.

She invited us to dinner in a restaurant where the prices filled us with terror, but she declared she was too rich to worry about such trifles. While we might have harboured doubts about her wealth, we could not doubt her generosity or her taste for luxury, but we did wonder where she had acquired it—in Moscow, where poverty was still universal?

At ten in the evening, the two of us were in her room at the Grand Hotel with a view of the Opéra and of a sea of cars, their mechanical yapping rising up to our floor. When we were lying in the large upholstered bed, she began her interrogation: 'So, you're a mannequin? I know what that is: I've seen collections presented in Berlin. You're well dressed—that's something, at least. But living in a maid's room! Dreadful!'

'I don't earn much,' I said.

'Who are you sleeping with?'

This is when things started to go wrong. I was tempted to lie, but I knew Gulnar's ear was too attuned to deception. No one knew it better than her and her brothers. She wouldn't be taken in. I resigned myself to the truth. 'I haven't got a lover.'

'Huh, you, you're not normal! How long have you been without a lover?'

I couldn't have felt more intimidated arraigned before a judge.

'Since I've been in Paris.' I felt awkward, ridiculous, stupid.

'God, what an idiot! Living in Paris, alone, free—our president told me you're thinking of getting a divorce—and denying yourself a lover.'

'I haven't denied myself anything. I don't want anyone.'

'She doesn't want anyone! As though wanting had anything to do with it. Oh, I'll have to sort this out!'

'Sort this out' were her final words for the evening. With the ease I had always envied, inclined as I was to insomnia, she fell asleep, leaving me alone in the night and wide awake. I could see our gardens on the Caspian where we grew up, she and I, her brothers and my sisters, in heat and abundance, in the shade of poplars and oleanders, flowering acacias and climbing jasmine which dazed us with their scent, surely the same as in paradise. I saw again the cold pools where we would swim to release the heat accumulated in our bodies, and the warm Caspian where we didn't dare to venture too far out. Did I regret this lost childhood? Hardly, or not at all, except for the beautiful sky, sea, flowers, trees, all things that one can find elsewhere and just as beautiful. I surprised myself at how easily and brutally I rejected my past. How could I do that?

A fly tricked by the ray of light coming in between the loosely drawn curtains buzzed near my ear, immobilizing time. It reminded me of afternoons of crushing heat in the country, when Gulnar and I would sleep in the cool of a shuttered room.

I had heard that insect hum so often and would hear it so many more times that, better than reason, it made me aware of the unity of my being throughout all the metamorphoses imposed by life, and continues to do so. This buzzing was my Proustian madeleine, my perpetual time.

It was almost dawn before I fell asleep.

The next day we made our double move with the help of a taxi driver whose regal bearing and handsome looks could have made him a prince, a favourite of Catherine the Great, had he been born at the right time. You will have realized I'm talking about a Russian, a real one—fair, guaranteed Slav and strikingly imposing. There's no need to talk of an extraordinary coincidence that had us hail a Russian; at that time a high percentage of taxi drivers were soldiers from the White Army, the remnants of which were spread across Paris.

We had placed him before he had even opened his mouth, his race was so clearly written on his face; we spoke Russian to him from the start and from the start he worshipped Gulnar, who began to flirt with him—and to exploit him. Though generous by nature, she loved to exploit others. It gave her a heightened sense of importance, or rather, power.

First, he moved all the suitcases, and there were plenty of them! Then we left for my fine building on the Champ de Mars, where I had to pack my cases, which took no more than a quarter of an hour, so meagre were my possessions. Gulnar waited for us in the taxi. I'd filled her in on the moods of our whimsical lift. In the fine colonnaded entrance, Colonel Nikolai Karpov, who had already introduced himself, clicking his heels together in the best tradition of his status, headed for the imposing lift of the masters. I had to stop him, blushing with shame. 'Not this way. We have to take the service stairs. My room is on the seventh floor.'

Now I blush with shame as I remember my state of mind at that time, which is best described by the title of Jane Austen's famous novel *Pride and Prejudice*. A state of mind even more stupid when faced with a taxi driver who was in the same boat as me, and knew as well as me the problems of émigrés, their often fruitless and pitiable efforts to adapt to a situation with multiple difficulties. Colonel Karpov adjusted to the circumstances in the blink of an eye.

'Oh, what can you do; rich today, poor tomorrow. The Lord giveth and the Lord taketh away, according to His will. We know a thing or two about it, you and I.'

I pushed the narrow door out into the courtyard and led this man of faith towards my lift, which seemed to be fast asleep in its wire cage. I slid the latticework door open and thought I saw the animal half open a displeased eye. The driver got into the cage.

'I'm going up on foot. The poor thing is very feeble and I hate lifts anyway.'

'What can you do, it's old age. We shall all grow old one day. We come into this world as babes and leave it as old codgers.'

Having uttered this incontestable truth, he pressed the button and the animal moved with a plaintive groan and began to climb, already disheartened. He'll never make it, I thought to myself, and followed the lift, not having to put in too much effort to keep up. At the fourth floor the lift stopped for a moment's reflection, then began a slow descent. I could hear Karpov crying, 'Ach, *bozhe moy*; my God, now it's going down. Can you see it?'

Yes, I could! 'Don't be afraid. It's very gentle. It will reach the bottom without doing you any harm. I told you it was old.'

'Ach, *bozhe moy*! What a monster!'

The driver's cries faded into the distance. I could hear the lift stop at the bottom followed by the noise of it moving off again. Nikolai Karpov had guts and determination. I sat on a stair to await the next stage in this juddering ride, expecting nothing good to come of it, but I was wrong. I had underestimated the force of military authority. The monster of a lift reached the seventh floor safe and sound.

An hour later my bits and pieces had been transported to the furnished apartment, where, after refusing any tip, the colonel courted Gulnar with vodka and *zakuski*.* He departed, his heart on fire, leaving us his address, as Gulnar was planning a housewarming or just a 'do', and the handsome colonel was to attend, with or without his taxi.

'And now,' she said, when we were alone at last, collapsed in our armchairs, 'our new life begins.'

*

A month later we had moved into a fine apartment on Avenue Michel-Ange, fine but empty. Gulnar didn't want to furnish it until the arrival of her 'husband' of the day, Otto von X, who was attending to his business affairs, which she described as 'colossal', somewhere between Elberfeld, Berlin, Warsaw and Moscow. She had met him in Moscow 'at the home of mutual friends', she said with an air of mystery, an encounter where a flash of lightning as 'colossal' as Otto's commercial affairs had thrown them into one another's arms. What was he doing in

---

* Hors d'oeuvres.

Moscow? He sold all kinds of machinery there, produced at his factories in Elberfeld. It was less clear what Gulnar was doing in Moscow; interpreter, translator, secretary, language teacher… It was equally unclear how Otto managed to get her out of Russia. She claimed he had married her, but I soon found that she had a Soviet passport (which she was in a hurry to change for a Nansen passport), so was not his legal wife. But who are we to quibble over such a minor detail. A gale of liberalism was sweeping across the West and the permissive society was already beginning to show.

Otto's letters were frequent, long and in three languages: German, Russian and French, agreeably and cleverly intertwined. Otto was German on his father's side, Russian on his mother's (who was a Princess Golitsyn, Gulnar added proudly), and had been raised by a French governess, so he spoke perfect French. To listen to Gulnar, he possessed every quality except one, which she didn't mention, but I soon guessed: he couldn't win her love. Poor Otto, how did I already know that she was preparing dark days for him? My guess was child's play actually. I knew Gulnar's volcanic temperament, her taste for adventure and her constant fickleness, though perhaps the latter was due to all her love affairs to date having been mistakes. One can always wonder whether a woman is flighty out of congenital need or because destiny has refused her an encounter with the One, the man who would meet all her expectations. We may add that this question of comparative philosophy can also apply to men.

While waiting for Otto and his bottomless wallet to arrive, Gulnar bought three divans, four chairs and an enormous refrigerator in which she kept her shoes, not to mention a kitchen table and a minimum of crockery so that we could eat at home.

Fortunately, the apartment had huge cupboards, which was what had convinced Gulnar to rent it.

'There's no happiness without cupboards,' she liked to say, and I knew she was right. There were perhaps cupboards with no happiness around them, but there was no happiness without cupboards.

Suitcases and trunks covered in various pieces of cloth provided some furnishing for the surprisingly large and empty apartment.

'We shall be happy here,' Gulnar told me the first evening, giving her charming, mischievous smile, when we sat facing one another in the kitchen eating a cold collation. 'You must leave your job, because there's Otto. He has enough money for two women.'

I had no intention of following her advice. Having only just gained my independence, I did not want to depend on this mysterious Otto who had been held up in Berlin and was hoping to join us soon. While we waited, his trilingual letters betrayed between the lines a steady increase in suspicion about Gulnar's behaviour. But he was wrong—for now. She was too busy discovering Paris and its shops, where the treasures of Aladdin called to her, all so expensive that she delayed their purchase until Otto and his wallet were available. She kept her list of desires, which also increased in parallel with Otto's jealousy, and waited impatiently for his arrival. She wasn't even thinking of being unfaithful to him at present, as she didn't have time. In the evening I would find her slumped on one of the three divans and listen to her complaining about her fatigue, the amount of shopping she had done, the objects noted down for future acquisition and, finally, the delay in Otto's joining her. A month had already passed and we were still waiting for him. So she bought another kitchen table and put it in the dining room, and casually hired a woman called Clémentine who spoke pompously and drank solidly. The more intoxicated she became, the more she liked to use pseudo-Racinian language. She served us diligently but never missed an opportunity to join our conversation. If we didn't touch a dish, she would declaim, 'These ladies are wrong: food nourishes not only the body but the mind. And the mind,' she would add, raising a solemn finger into the air, 'is a great thing.'

'Oh yes, Clémentine, it is!' Gulnar would interrupt her, adding in Russian or Azeri, 'What an idiot!'

We were all burning with curiosity to see the mysterious Otto, whom Gulnar described as a genial businessman, an arbiter of elegance, the quintessence of a good education. According to her, he made millions, without specifying whether this was in dollars or the devalued marks, and I was wary of her oriental imagination anyway. But we had to admit that she was spending a lot of money and did have some beautiful jewellery.

At last, after another month of waiting, a telegram announced the arrival of Otto, this man who flew like a swallow from country to country. When I returned that very evening, I finally set eyes on him: a large man, with quite a fine face spoilt by jowls that wobbled when he spoke. A bird of prey's beak for a nose and a generous stomach gave him the classic air of a businessman. Yes, he was elegant and distinguished, he smelt discreetly good like an empty perfume bottle, and he greeted me like a brother, paying me a thousand compliments and expressing his satisfaction that his dear Gulnar had me for company. She had told him of my 'virtue' (I wondered in what tone: mocking, resigned, admiring?). The poor man was perhaps hoping that some of it would rub off on my fickle cousin. Despite his age and experience, he forgot the other possibility: Gulnar's influence on me. But he must have given me the qualities of a guardian angel and the fortitude to resist the worst temptation.

His jealousy tormented him like a latent illness. In the morning he would spend two hours washing and grooming, and would also use the time for his daily round of suspicion. He would walk from bathroom to bedroom and back again, razor or comb in hand or brandishing his nail file or toothbrush covered in Nab, a powder for scouring washbasins that he did not hesitate to use as toothpaste, claiming that nothing else was as effective.

Still half-asleep, her pretty head resting graciously on a silk pillow, Gulnar would make soothing noises to calm Otto's combative ardour, which was gradually subsiding and would make a final retreat.

'How can a man of your quality be so basely jealous?' Gulnar would ask, an expression of saintly charity on her impish face.

'Oh, my dear, it's stronger than me,' Otto would hastily respond, reassured by these two hours of suspicions—as yet unfounded, but not for much longer.

'I love you so much.'

It would end in tender kisses and very good lunches in town, almost always with me, whom they would come to find at the Place Vendôme.

When he was not prey to jealousy Otto was charming, very generous, and had an indefatigable desire to indulge us. Like Gulnar, he encouraged me to leave my job—'It's so beneath you'—but I paid no heed to these two sirens. Not only was I preserving my independence, I was concerned about Gulnar's whims, as she might decide at any time that she had already loved Otto for too long. She was convinced that prolonged fidelity 'clogged up' the body and the heart and would end in disgust. 'You cannot eat the same dish, however exquisite, every day for years.'

Though I was still working, my life had changed considerably: farewell the seventh floor, so sad and poor, the ageing lift, and what was after all a solitary existence. It was so lovely to return to the fine apartment, which was gradually being furnished in a more than respectable fashion, to enter my bright room with a view over a courtyard garden, to eat a good dinner, Gulnar always smiling and glad to see me. Every day, I thanked fate for sending me my cousin and now Otto, whom every day I appreciated more and more, lamenting the time he would be replaced; good heavens, by whom? But why be sad in advance? It would be too stupid.

Otto spent a whole month with us, satisfying Gulnar in every way he could and spoiling me too; a real horn of plenty that showered us with gifts and pleasures, bounty of every kind. Inter alia, he spent a small fortune in Russian nightclubs, which Gulnar loved and he put up with in order to please her; though didn't he enjoy them just a little, thinking of his late mother, Princess Golitsyn, thanks to whom Russian blood flowed abundantly in his veins? On his last evening we decided unanimously to take a final dip into the distinctive ambience of a Russian nightclub.

'In those days', even the fustiest of Parisians knew those establishments, as they were dotted all over the capital. They exuded a noble melancholy, but anyone who looks for this legendary atmosphere today will be disappointed. It has disappeared, after half a century of exile. Who could recreate it? They have almost all disappeared, the émigrés who were the former lords of the earth, bearers of tradition, those who, overwhelmed by exile, loved to evoke a dead past through Russian Gypsy songs imported from home. The ballads dripped with nostalgia, which, like some remedies, is both good and bad for you, fanning the flames of despair but releasing a suppressed sadness. The young émigrés have forgotten this subtle art of finding enjoyment in the skilful expression of sadness. To have fun and to despair; to drink, shed a tear from the corner of your eye and laugh from the corner of your mouth; to tear your guts out at the recollection of the great shipwreck, but tuck into your supper; to drink again and sing again and cry again: this was the programme of the Russian nightclubs, eagerly enjoyed by natives and tourists from both hemispheres, to the great detriment of their wallets. In fact, the expense could be justified by the uniqueness of these places, where one bathed in an exquisite atmosphere of exoticism and Parisianism, of Siberian steppes and Veuve Clicquot, of the white nights of St Petersburg and sword dances, of supremely elegant women and lamb skewers known as shashlik.

I don't know any more which Caucasian castle or cellar or barrel we entered that night. All I remember is the Caucasian part of the name. Otto took us there because his loving heart cherished anything Caucasian.

He chose a recessed table, to Gulnar's great disappointment, as she was dying to be on display in a place where we might meet acquaintances, to show off her stunning flame-red velvet dress and her jewellery, which all enhanced her distinctive charm. But she knew from experience that Otto was doing this for the sake of respectability. One did not take young women from good families to a nightclub. But there he was, poor thing, infinitely touching in his innocence from another age. Gulnar was kind enough not to shatter his illusions.

So we sat at our secluded table, from which we could still see the orchestra, the singers and a good number of the audience. The maître d'hôtel came to take our order as though he were doing us a favour as a result of unfortunate circumstances, which was in fact historically accurate. Like all the nightclub staff, his social class was overwhelming to customers who were commoners; the others adapted to it. What title other than a noble one had he held in Russia: senator, Marshal of Nobility, chamberlain to Nicholas II or something higher?

The evening, or rather the night, was just beginning, and the opening acts, the second-rate ones according to custom, were still on stage. A plump lady was dutifully singing an interminable song, though nobody was listening. When she finished, some kind customers applauded, so the lady grabbed the opportunity to start another. When she'd finished her insipid crooning, the orchestra struck up some jazz. This gave me a flashback.

I dreaded this music at the start of my Parisian life, and shrank from its beat like Alice in Wonderland; I became a child again in Baku, I could hear a boom-boom similar to the sound of an American jazz orchestra, but it was a drumbeat of mourning. It accompanied a procession of men naked to the waist who moved slowly, beating their backs with small chains of razor-sharp iron attached to a stick. Torches illuminated hundreds of penitents who were flagellating themselves to the same slow rhythm beaten out by the tom-tom, and crying at the same time, 'Sha Hossein, va Hossein.' Blood streamed down, but the men, in a trance, ignored it, striking their wounds all the more. A collective mysticism transports them, inebriates them, detaches them from their bodies, which they are mortifying in order to atone for the death of the holy Imam Hossein, son of Fatima, grandson of the

Prophet, murdered in a cowardly fashion along with his family at Kerbala, which has since become a Shia holy city.

I must have been eight years old when my grandmother, wanting to instruct me in Islam, had the bad idea of taking me to the mosque to witness up close the mortification of good Muslims. In the lattice-screened lodges reserved for women the overheated atmosphere filled me with anxiety, making me want to escape right away. On top of his minbar (an elevated chair for sermons) the mullah was preaching on or reading the Koran; I don't know which, as all I could hear was a confused noise augmented by the ringing in my ears; slow at first, then faster and faster, the sound of metal hitting the backs of the penitents, the noise of the chains gouging their flesh accompanied by their cries of *'Sha Hossein, va Hossein.'* The women, confined to their lodges, begin to tear at the shawls covering their heads, then at their hair; their ardour growing in time with the men's, they beat their heads against the wall and scratch their skin with their fingernails. Finding their chains too soft, some fanatics grab daggers that have appeared out of nowhere and slash their flesh. A tempest is unleashed, of sweat, blood, clamour, insanity, and this madness is charging towards me; I feel the chains, the daggers, the nails digging into me; I yell, I try to run out of the lodge, someone holds me back, I lose consciousness…

We're a long way from the Caucasian castle or cellar or barrel, and I return with a sigh of relief. The jazz tom-tom has stopped and a group of handsome Slavs is singing. What can a group of handsome Slavs sing, if not 'The Volga Boatmen', which at that time was just at the start of its career? And what can genuine Gypsies, their authenticity guaranteed on the astronomical bill, sing, if not 'The Two Guitars'? These two famous songs were as integral a part of the Russian emigration as the famous cabbage soup borsch, grand dukes, endemic ill will towards the host countries and internal quarrels.

> Speak to me, please,
> Seven-stringed guitar.
> You satisfy my soul,
> While the moon shines bright

howled the Gypsy from her heart, or as they say in Russian, 'her chest', her voice rising from the depths of her being. She ripped out our guts, instilled in us a sense of the ultimate void and gave us a taste of death. Then the chorus came in, surrounding and supporting the soloist; six or seven male voices cried together, and the guitarists pounded their instruments with the flats of their palms, together creating a thunderous frenzy around the repeating chords, but getting faster all the time, more violent, intended to throw you off balance, to make you want to pull off the tablecloth with all the glasses and bottles, or join the crazy ululation of the singers, or perform a wild dance. Finally, the uproar stopped and something approaching order was restored, though with noticeably increased perspiration, nostalgia and nervous tension. The understanding management distributed paper fans to keep us in the land of the living.

The club was now packed to the rafters, as there was a never-ending stream of new admirers of Russian nostalgia. The clientele that night was especially Parisian, that is to say, cosmopolitan. We saw an oriental potentate celebrated for his fortune and his corpulence, both considerable; an English lord with a famous name; the most beautiful woman in Paris, kept in splendour by a Peruvian billionaire; the most extravagant American woman in Europe; and others, many others. The club soon resembled a life raft overflowing with humanity, with newcomers sent away to other, less fashionable clubs. Piled on top of one another, sweating so much that fans were no help, dying of a thirst that the most expensive champagne could not quench, physically uncomfortable, mixing chairs, legs and curiosity, the revellers were resolved to get their money's worth, a heroic determination that was visible to all. People shuffled on their chairs, drank, laughed, shrieked to make themselves heard in the hubbub, and when they were let loose they charged to the narrow dance floor, so crowded they had to dance on the spot, each dancer hanging on to their corner so as not to be dislodged. But they were not disheartened and continued jumping on the spot with a youthful elan that bore no relation to age. An old American lady decked in jewels capered about clasped in the arms of a handsome young man, whom I recognized as a Georgian prince known for his skill as a seducer of the rich. Gulnar and Otto took a few steps at the edge of the dance floor. He couldn't take his eyes off her, while she was very much the grande dame way above the common fray. I envied her grace, her piquant prettiness, her skill at living her life. I wanted to slip into her skin, but I knew that once I was inside her, she would become me, with all the psychological burdens, anxiety and insecurity that I dragged around with me. Alone at my table, I daydreamed—about what? Happiness. What happiness? Love, of course—great, vast, eternal.

★

Otto was on edge on the station platform, where we had both gone to see him off: his jowls were pale and the lines on his face revealed the extent of his anxiety. He was almost thirty years older than Gulnar, and suddenly I could see them weighing on him, on his greying temples, on the creases at the corner of his mouth, on the bags under his eyes. Anxiety highlighted them dramatically. He was suffering from jealousy, doubts gnawing away at him.

'My dear, promise me you'll be faithful during this month or two. Promise to write to me often and tell me everything.'

Gulnar frowned impatiently, but remembered herself. 'Yes, of course, of course, we've talked about this a hundred times. It gets so tiring!'

'You need to understand—' Otto replied, but she interrupted him again.

'I understand. I understand only too well this masculine obsession with having exclusive rights to us.' When she saw the panic on Otto's face, she changed her tone again. 'I'm sorry. I'm just so stressed by you leaving that I don't know what I'm saying any more. I can assure you I'm going to miss you cruelly. I love you much more than you think.'

Poor Otto's jowls turned pink. He needed so little to be happy—just a few lies, which are often a good thing, it seems to me, kind and dictated by the desire to spare injury. I was grateful to Gulnar for this gesture and resolved to encourage her in this vein. Otto took her in his arms and covered her with passionate kisses. I was so torn by pity for him that I turned away lest I burst into tears. He boarded his carriage, the train whistle sounded, the guards shouted; he waved his white handkerchief for a long time, until the handkerchief, the carriage, then the train itself faded away.

In the taxi home Gulnar drew up a plan of action to 'celebrate' the departure, as she said cruelly. Otto had left her a large sum in the bank, and liberty reclaimed and amply gilded had to be exploited without delay. She planned to give a party at the Josézous's, as she thought their studio and its bohemian atmosphere better suited for the celebration, which she wanted to make as unconventional as possible. After this month spent in Otto's arms, so good but so encumbered by propriety, she was longing for novelty and above all pleasure of a particular kind. She already knew with whom she would find it: Colonel Nikolai Karpov, whom she had filed away in her memory for the day of her liberation.

'He will be my *zakuski* while I wait for the *pièce de résistance* that will come along one day.'

'Poor Otto, who's just—'

'Oh no, no virtuous compassion, please. I've just given him a priceless month of my youth and it was deadly dull, so I owe him nothing. And as for you, you should watch your step. Since you're so apathetic, I'm going to have to find you a lover. It can't go on like this.'

Since I'd become the incarnation of chastity, she saw me as a living reproach, always before her eyes, a killjoy who needed to be brought back to normal life. I protested, but feebly, not knowing what I wanted, reading myself so badly: irresolute, prey to doubt, desire, fear.

The Josézous acquiesced with enthusiasm to Gulnar's request to hold a Liberation Party; they put at her disposal their studio, themselves, their friends, their time and their efforts. So she sent out invitations and placed sumptuous orders with caterers, both French and Russian. There were to be some fifty guests, who would be fed and watered royally. She didn't skimp on either the quantity or the quality of the food and drink to celebrate her deliverance.

*

Almeria's was the first face I saw when I made my way into the studio, artfully decorated as an artist's home should be. He wore an expression of such pathos that it was indecent in its raw nakedness. He had fallen for Gulnar at their first meeting; it was an unhappy love, of course, as his filthy appearance ruled out his candidacy, though she did find some attraction in such a passionate nature. 'I might be able to sleep with Almeria if he boiled himself in a sterilizer. But then what would be left of him?'

Short at the best of times, sorrow had shrunk him and unassuaged passion was ravaging his features. He stared at Gulnar in a daze, without daring to court her, but that look, my God, it smouldered and almost caught fire! I didn't think my cousin had ever seemed so desirable: the intensity of her being, her lust for life, her taste for love gave her the air of a bacchanal without convention or calculation, a woman in her original state, nothing but a woman, but so totally, so perfectly a woman that all men desired her. How drab I felt beside her, able at best to make her bed, where she would behave like a queen, she who had faith in the invincible language of the body, a language I had never known. Achieve victory, but what victories could I win with my poor, dull resources? I sat in a corner of the studio, depressed, envious of the happiness of others, and watched proceedings.

The guests stood around a long table, created out of trestles but covered with a magnificent tablecloth bought specially for the occasion by Gulnar. They ate and drank without flagging. Ivan Petrovich was so soaked in alcohol that the least pressure on his flesh might cause it to swell up like a balloon. A small glass of vodka was all it took for him to savour the delights of inebriation. His gaze expressed the dumb gaiety typical of inveterate drinkers. Enlivening his tale with gestures, he recounted how he had one day stopped runaway horses that were leading equipage and passengers on a crazy ride towards death. And not just passengers, but female passengers—he had saved some grand duchesses!

'When you see runaway horses pounding towards you, you hurry—'

'Oh, that's too fascinating!' cried an incredulous or polite Frenchman, a lawyer named Jérôme de Labusserie, whom Michel Murat had brought along for the first time. 'How did they express their gratitude?'

'The tsar did it in person, at the Winter Palace. What could he do? He couldn't pay me, after all, as I'm from a better family than him—older and just as rich, or we used to be. But he thanked me with extraordinary warmth. The empress too.'

'Drink this and shut up,' Shamsi said in Russian, to avoid embarrassing him in front of a Frenchman. They had studied together at the same school in St Petersburg, which accepted only noblemen with x degrees of nobility. 'Talk about a tall tale.'

And he handed him a glass of vodka, which Ivan Petrovich accepted gratefully. This party *à la russe* required the guests to be brought to the proper level of inebriation, something that Shamsi was good at. He ordered (yes, ordered) General Tzavidze, who had naturally brought his guitar, to sing a drinking song in honour of each guest. The appointed victim would knock back in one the glass of vodka proffered with great ceremony by one of the ladies. In order to show their familiarity with the customs of the boyars some guests smashed their glasses on the floor after draining them. Everyone applauded, including the hosts. With these barbaric customs in mind, they had bought the cheapest glasses in Paris, and all breakages were included in the cost of the party.

Happy to have been forgiven all his social failings, José submitted to Shamsi's dominance with touching good will. Watching him drink vodka Russian-style, I imagined him more at home in a snowed-in Russian *izba* than a Castilian village. He had learnt a fine variety of Russian and Azeri obscenities and two drinking songs, and he would rather have borsch than any European soup. In Russian restaurants he would call for the *shiotte* with a knowing air, which tended to cause confusion because of his poor pronunciation, the Russian accent being difficult for foreigners. He should have said *s-chot,* which not everyone can manage.

Condescending and very much the grand seigneur at ease with his serfs, Shamsi treated his brother in-law with a haughty benevolence and would even consent to borrow small sums from him which he always forgot to return and which José did not dare ask for, especially since Zuleykha was in the dark about it and would not have approved.

When he thought the guests sufficiently inebriated, he decreed there would be choral singing, a Russian obsession that I hated. They always sang the same endless songs. But unfortunately tradition is not to be questioned, and anyway, I was overcome with sadness that evening and did not care.

Tatiana, a painter friend of Zuleykha's, sang louder and more out of tune than the others, but she was so beautiful she was forgiven. Beautiful, very Slav, slightly dotty, she painted pictures that were also mad, though with religious inspiration. She painted cubist icons and annunciations with a carnival atmosphere. Her deep faith dictated her entire conduct. For example, one night when she was in bed in the loft of her two-storey studio, she heard burglars forcing the front door, and telephoned her priest rather than the police. Her cleric, more practical, alerted the nearest police station. She often refused to take payment for her icons: 'Why, you will pay me in the other world,' she would say, with deep conviction and no affectation.

In another way she resembled Almeria: she was distinctly slovenly. Her clothes were held up by pins and prayers. Strands of unwashed blonde hair straggled her face of a Madonna, barely touched by make-up, which we abused outrageously at that time.

'Look at my Renaissance shadows,' she liked to say, and no one objected, as they weren't quite sure what quattrocento shadows were.

Nikolai Karpov sang with brio, sensing his chances with Gulnar. Despite his badly cut jacket, which he still managed to wear with panache, everyone was taken with him, even Shamsi. He seemed to be an utter fool, but that's of no great concern to an inebriated group of partygoers. He had only two topics of conversation: his military career, cut short by the revolution, and his adventures as a taxi driver. His luminous beauty—hair, complexion, teeth, eyes—shone more than ever that evening, as he felt himself in a state of favour.

Gulnar's other suitor, Almeria, suffered from loving too much and not being loved in return. Gulnar paid him no attention, and when he happened to be in her line of vision she would quickly turn away. If he came up to her, she would demonstratively turn her back on him, and alcohol was his only recourse in the face of her cruelty.

Towards midnight, Almeria had had a skinful, one might say. Looking pathetic, he was standing not far from Nikolai Karpov and playing with the Castilian grandfather's famous sword, when suddenly he walked up to the Russian, brandishing the weapon with the clear intention of thrusting it into him. Had he forgotten he was dealing with a colonel? It was child's play for a smiling Nikolai Karpov to snatch the sword off him and return it to José, who put it back in its sheath. This humiliation was the final straw for Almeria. He ran out of the studio, head in hands.

Someone was keeping a watchful, benevolent eye on what to him was a new drama: Jérôme de Labusserie, Murad's guest. A few subtle compliments put him in Gulnar's good books and she invited him to visit us, which he accepted eagerly. He lacked neither intuition nor sensitivity, as he discerned my dejection and tried to snap me out of it—unsuccessfully. I take no pride in confessing that the more Gulnar shone, the more I froze, feeling doomed to the role of eternal onlooker.

I didn't know that Jérôme de Labusserie's future friendship with the two of us would have an unexpected influence on my life.

The party also ushered in a period of *amour à la russe* between Gulnar and Nikolai Karpov, who had no idea that the conceit of his new mistress was a flame that would burn his wings.

Since we are entering the Russian period, it is time that I wrote a few words, or a few pages, about the emigration to which Gulnar and I were attached, not by race, but by association with the Empire of the Tsars.

White Emigration in the Wake of the October Revolution

Some may find it flippant, perhaps in bad taste, to begin this chapter about what is essentially a tragedy with an ironic story by the Russian author Teffi. Herself an émigré in France, she was all too familiar with the plight of the displaced. But tragedy is rarely not interlaced with comedy, so, reluctant to overwhelm the reader from the outset, I have chosen as an introduction this sardonic text entitled 'The Small Town':

It was a town of forty thousand inhabitants, with a church and countless taverns. [I have to make a correction here: there were many churches, not just one, though they weren't as numerous as the taverns.]

A brook ran through it. In olden times it was called the Sequana, then the Seine, and when the town grew up around it the inhabitants called it 'their little Neva'.

The population lived at close quarters, either in a suburb named Passy or on 'Theleftbank'.

Most young people worked in transport and became drivers. Mature men ran taverns or were employed by them, the darker-haired as Gypsies or Caucasians, the fair as Little Russians.

The women ran up dresses and hats for one another. The men ran up debts.

As well as men and women, the townsfolk included ministers and generals. Few of them worked in transport; most were busy incurring debts and writing their memoirs.

The memoirs had the aim of glorifying their author and shaming their compatriots. The memoirs differed in that some were written by hand, while others were typed.

Time passed in a very monotonous fashion.

A theatre sometimes came to the town and showed lively dinner plates and dancing clocks. The citizens demanded free tickets, but were spiteful about the performances. The management distributed free seats and were slowly crushed by the triumphant insults of the public.

There was also a newspaper in the town which everyone wanted to receive free of charge, but the paper stood up for itself and survived. [Another correction here: there were several newspapers, not just one.]

People were not much interested in public affairs. They met under the sign of Russian borsch, but in small groups, as they hated one another so much that if twenty people came together, ten would be the sworn enemies of the other ten. If by chance they weren't, they soon would be.

The town was oddly situated, surrounded not by fields, forests or valleys, but by the streets of the most glittering capital in the world, with marvellous museums, galleries and theatres. But the townsfolk did not mix with those of the capital and did not enjoy the fruits of this foreign civilization. They even had their own shops.

The townsfolk spoke a strange argot, in which philologists could easily trace Slavic roots. The townsfolk liked to hear that one of their own was a thief, a swindler or a traitor. They also liked curd cheese and long telephone conversations. They were very bad-tempered and never laughed.

Humourless émigrés reproached Teffi for this satirical tale, while others laughed. The author was blessed with a lively intelligence and suffered as much as anyone from the 'truly grandiose and tragic phenomenon' of emigration. She considered humour an antidote to the painful condition of the exile and had no compunction about using it. The definition of emigration that I have just given is by Ivan Bunin, the first Russian to receive the Nobel Prize in literature, who also emigrated to France, where he lived for many years in obscurity, interrupted only by a brief interval of fame owing to the prize. The small sum that he received did not last as long as the recipient, and he died in poverty. As for Teffi, she died of heart disease, alone and in semi-destitution. She confessed to me once that she would seek shelter in a post office to escape the sense of abandonment and to feel connected to humanity, if only in a derisory fashion.

'The small town', as Teffi called it, wasn't all that small. It didn't consist of forty thousand inhabitants, but twice, if not three or four times, that number. People lived according to clan, class and especially the ethnicities that created the colourful mosaic of the Russian Empire, and that create the same mosaic of the Soviet Union.

The huge region of my native Caucasus alone provided a

considerable contingent of Georgians, Armenians, Azerbaijanis, Ossetians, Circassians and Chechens, to whom were added Ukrainians, Crimean Tatars and Gypsies from all the regions, Balts, many of them of German origin, and finally Russians. This disparate society formed a diverse mass—whose only common denominator was the loss of homeland, nationality, property and social status. Had one been able to bring together in a specially selected location all the émigrés scattered around the world, one would have created an offshoot of the Russian Empire detached from its main trunk. It was a curious phenomenon that did not escape the notice of many contemporaries, including the American Chapin-Huntington, who wrote in 1933 that

> Among the war-born nations there is one which appears in no atlas, no yearbook. Yet it has a population of one million, probably the most highly educated in the world... It has no government, but its capital is Paris... its colonies are scattered throughout the world.
>
> One half of the population are ex-soldiers, but it has no standing army. No parliament here... yet we see a very rainbow of parties representing all shades of political conviction, from monarchism to socialism—except communism...
> These people strive to maintain a far-flung school system, in order that the young shall not forget the noble language and splendid traditions of their ancestors... Every sixth man has a university diploma and two-thirds of the population are high-school graduates...*

---

* *The Homesick Million: Russia-out-of-Russia*, The Stratford Company, Boston (MA), 1933.

How many of them were there? We will never know, as very different figures have been put forward. Some seem to have been plucked out of the air, as there are no reliable sources. According to Paul A. Ladame, there must have been two million of them (*Le rôle des migrations dans le monde libre*, 'The role of migration in the free world', Librairies H. Droz, Geneva, 1958). Soviet statistics make the same estimate. The German Von Rimscha gives the higher figure of 2,935,000 people (*Russland jenseits der Grenzen*, 'Russia beyond its borders', Jena, 1927). According to V. Abdank-Kossovsky, they numbered between eight and ten million…

In reality, no one can give an exact number, or at least that's my impression. This is for several reasons, most obviously the, in many cases, highly fluid nature of the departures, or, to be more exact, escapes. Russia is vast, and for those who crossed its borders to the north, south, east or west, often in dramatic circumstances, one's civil status counted for very little, if anything at all—it was expedient to make up a status at that time, especially in countries such as China, Manchuria or Persia, where administration was not as highly regulated as in the West.

Many Russian women married nationals of the countries where they found themselves, and did not appear on any list of refugees. Some émigrés had financial means and tended to acquire a nationality that suited them, thereby avoiding refugee status. In fact, the émigrés who later had the right to Nansen passports were a long way from representing emigration in its entirety. So to give a precise figure is in the realms of science fiction. Imagine, for a moment, the exodus created by the revolution:

Nobles, politicians, intellectuals, soldiers, the pursued, the privileged of all kinds, the whole mass of people seeking to flee a country drowning in blood and mired in civil war and famine, all tried to cross the cordon sanitaire separating a Russia in flames from the rest of the world where the war had only just finished. They crossed borders under rifle and sub-machinegun fire, swam across rivers, walked over mountain passes, slipped beneath barbed wire, braved the deserts of Central Asia or the frozen forests of Siberia, boarded ship in Novorossiysk, Odessa, Arkhangelsk, Vladivostok or Batumi. Thousands of kilometres of borders witnessed their passage, struggling, running and dying beneath the bullets, or reaching at last their desired goal. They fled.

With every new defeat of the White armies, the soldiers of Kolchak, Denikin, Wrangel and Petliura joined the civilian refugees, swelling the torrent that flowed towards the land or maritime borders.

This tidal wave flooded Europe, its first breakers buffeting Constantinople, the Balkans, the Nordic countries, then reaching further, ever further. Ravaged, impoverished France, scarcely emerged from a murderous war, received around half a million émigrés, most of them penniless and many without a profession. The whole of Europe was talking about them and not always charitably, for there were too many of them, they were everywhere. There were between two and four hundred thousand émigrés in defeated Germany, which was a hundred times more wretched than France and was struggling with a rate of inflation inconceivable today. They converged on Berlin, clustering near the Tiergarten. 'The Russians circle around the old church in Berlin like flies around a chandelier,' said the writer Shklovsky.

England received them in dribs and drabs.

It is worth recalling an interesting episode here, unique in European history: after a Soviet decree issued in October 1921 stripped the émigrés of their nationality, hundreds of thousands of them lost their legal existence. It was Nansen, appointed president of the High Commission for Refugees, who found a solution to this new juridical problem: on the 3rd of July 1922, during a conference organized on his initiative in Geneva, sixteen states adopted his plan for an identity certificate which later became known the world over as a 'Nansen passport'. The refugees regained legal status, and could ask the League of Nations for help. Many contemporaries thought this a brilliant innovation.

'It may seem bizarre to talk of the Nansen passport as a "brilliant idea",' wrote Paul A. Ladame, whom I've already cited, 'when today, aid for refugees encompasses far more important issues. But it should not be forgotten that at that time governments had no idea of the scope of the problem or their responsibility in this regard.'

We should also mention in passing that today, many working migrants try to obtain the status of political refugee, as it confers advantages that they do not have as economic immigrants.

*

Ivan Bunin was right to maintain that the emigration resulting from the October Revolution was a 'truly grandiose and tragic phenomenon'.

Some mentioned the Jewish diaspora in this regard, but this was partly religious in nature and had stretched over millennia.

Others compared it to the French emigration after the 1789 revolution, but the difference between them is enormous, first in terms of size, and second in terms of composition. The majority of the French émigrés belonged to the nobility, the privileged of the Ancien Régime, and constituted a far less complex social phenomenon, while Russian emigration included all social classes: from the simple soldier loyal to his tsar to grand dukes; from the prima ballerina to the peasant enlisted in the White Army; from intellectuals to generals, including artists and servants who came with their deposed masters. Thus, this imaginary Russia-outside-of-Russia was composed of all its ethnicities and all its ancient orders, in the Russian sense of the word: the orders of the nobility, merchants, petite bourgeoisie, peasants, clergy, etc.

How to list all the stars studding the Russian diaspora? Can any statistician work out what percentage of the émigrés were celebrities? It's impossible to cite them all, here at any rate. Professor P.E. Kovalevsky* who tried to do so, must have come in for criticism from many sides for his omissions. In their merely 'phantom' capital, Paris, there were dozens of illustrious names, whom I list off the top of my head: Chaliapin, Stravinsky, Prokofiev,† and the prima ballerina Kschessinska—the former mistress of Nicholas II, she owned a palace that the Bolsheviks used for their congresses at the start of the revolution; she later married a grand duke. She ran a ballet school at Passy, which I even visited once to admire this woman still full of grace and

---

* *La Russie hors des frontières* ('Russia beyond its borders'), Vol. I and II, Librairie des Cinq Continents, Paris.
† Stravinsky later settled in the USA while Prokofiev returned to Russia.

agility at sixty. Preobrajenska and Balashova were stars like her but not married to grand dukes, as far as I know.

There were Russian writers aplenty in Paris: Bunin, Teffi, Remizov, Merezhkovsky and his wife Gippius, Kuprin (who returned to Russia in 1937, where he died a year later), Zaytsev, Adamovich...

The poets V. Ivanov, Marina Tsvetaeva, Balmont, Severyanin...

As Kovalevsky writes, 'Russian emigration in the so-called "pre-war" period (1920–39) created its most important and richest cultural centre in Paris in the early 1920s.'

The cultural forces included philosophers and theologians such as Berdyaev, Shestov, Lossky and Bulgakov.

There were dozens of painters—Kandinsky, Chagall, Tereshkovich, Bakst, etc.—and figures from the theatrical world—Balieff, the Pitoëffs, Evreïnoff, etc. How to name them all? We can give only an approximate idea of the extraordinary abundance of talent, exiled for political or other reasons. It goes without saying that on the whole the emigration was more on the 'right'.

The poet Mayakovsky, who made a trip to Europe in 1922, wrote this on the subject: 'The fiercest, so-called "ideological", emigration is to be found in Paris: Merezhkovsky, Gippius, Bunin, and others. There's no filth they don't dump on anything to do with Soviet Russia.'

One wonders if he felt at ease in this new Russia, which he himself left in another sort of emigration—suicide.

A dozen members of the Tolstoy family also lived in Paris. At first they were as poor as church mice, so poor that when the film *Anna Karenina* was shown in Paris in the 1920s, the author's daughter Tatiana Sukhotina-Tolstaya could not afford to go and see it.

The celebrated Prince Yusupov, who added the title of Rasputin's murderer to that of prince, and was furthermore married to Nicholas II's niece, opened a couture house in Paris named Irfé (from Irina and Félix, their first names).

I knew the house well, as I worked there as second saleswoman for a few months, but without having the chance to meet the princely couple, who were said to be extremely handsome.

A bouquet of grand dukes increased the glamour of these refugees. They all set to work like common peasants. One even became a taxi driver. I've already mentioned another, who married the ballerina Kschessinska—without ulterior motive, it should be said, though it made good business sense, since his wife ran a flourishing school. A duchess became a professional photographer, something perfectly respectable today. We know a gentleman of that profession who is married to a royal princess, but one did not do this back then.

It may be assumed, a little arbitrarily but not without reason, that two-thirds of the Russian diaspora were intimately acquainted with the life of the displaced at its lowest level. They were victims of the failure to adapt, either through lack of preparation for a working life, or through bad luck, or through a psychological incapacity to disengage from their culture in order to engage with another, with its very different way of life and mode of being.

Deeply unhappy, the émigrés pined for the homeland, though it was a homeland that no longer existed as they had known it. Teffi told me once that she did not see her Russia as a territory planted with silver birches or as the streets of St Petersburg, but as a cultural and social entity that had disappeared.

'What would I do there?' she asked in the spirit of the times. This did not stop her suffering in France, though, like so many of her compatriots who enlighten us on the subject. In his article 'Homeland', Kuprin described the different forms of homesickness, ending with these lines:

> The sickness is no longer acute, but chronic. One lives in a fine country (France), among the monuments of a high civilization, but everything is unreal, as though one were watching a film unfold… And there comes a dull, silent ache from no longer dreaming in one's sleep of Moscow or Russia; a black hole gapes in their place.

In his 'Letter from Paris', the poet Balmont writes with melancholy: 'Now, the further I go down foreign roads, the further my ties with my homeland come undone.'

Prokofiev thought himself too Russian to find inspiration abroad. In the 1920s, Rachmaninov said in an interview with an American journalist, 'Having abandoned Russia, I've lost all desire to compose. With my homeland lost, I've also lost my self.'

The great poet Marina Tsvetaeva held another point of view at first: 'Homeland is not determined by territory, it is the immutability of memory and blood. Only he who thinks of Russia as external from himself can fear no longer being Russian or forgetting Russia. Whoever carries it within him will lose it only when he dies…' Later, she must have decided that carrying it within her did not suffice. She returned.

The writer Bunin, who had the most brilliant 'success' in exile, always suffered from having been uprooted, though he refused to return to his country despite invitations from the

Soviets. When I voiced my surprise, he said, 'They will want to make me say what I don't think, oblige me to believe what I refuse to believe.'

There is a majesty of soul in a poor old man—the Nobel prize having long since been 'eaten'—who refuses material well-being and honours, of which he was fond, when they are placed within his reach.

Refusing to return at the same time as refusing to integrate or simply to make friendships—what am I saying, simply to make contact with the French people—such was the state of mind of the great majority of the Russian intelligentsia. They lived among themselves in a virtual ghetto of their own making. Hardly any acknowledged their own responsibility for this, instead blaming the 'natives', their inhospitality, their aloofness, which was often real on an individual level but false on a national level, France being a country that has always received large numbers of political refugees from all over the world. Might it be that this excess of foreigners eventually turned the French away from them? It's not impossible.

As far as I am concerned, the French have welcomed me and invited me for long visits so often that it would be ungracious not to mention it here. One might object that my status as a writer has opened many doors to me, a result of the rampant literary mania endemic in France. But Teffi and Bunin (a winner of the Nobel Prize in Literature to boot!) also enjoyed the same flattering status, yet complained just as much of being subject to a sort of ostracism. Did they really want to be free of it? I doubt it. Even speaking French seemed like a constraint to them.

In fact, it seems that the majority of Russians do not take well to the French (and by extension Western) mentality, which is based on order, thrift and, in France, that famous 'aloofness'. Madeleine Doré, who has produced a study on the issue* is quite right to say that they hold on to their nationalism, a feeling exacerbated by their displacement, while integration appears to them a betrayal of their homeland.

She adds that even naturalized, they continue to feel eminently Russian and assimilate badly. We should not forget that these remarks apply in particular to first-generation emigrants; the second generation is already highly 'contaminated' by the ambient psychological climate, while the third no longer has any integration problem.

Naturalization was rare between 1919 and 1941: of 532,868 Russians in France, only 18,973 became naturalized. Mixed marriages, again according to Madeleine Doré, were common among the working classes and rarer in the middle classes. In 1930 and 1931 there were 6,055, of which 5,269 were between Russian men and French women.

'The mere fact that the men are far more numerous than the women (the ratio is two or three to one),' writes Madeleine Doré, 'is not enough to explain this phenomenon. The Russian woman appears to be less Francophile than the Russian man and cares little for the French man.'

My personal observation, spanning over half a century, points in exactly the same direction: I have often heard Russian men speak 'as French patriots', never the women. I would, however, like to protect myself from the vice of generalization, which

---

* Institut National d'Études Démographiques, *Cahier no. 1: Les travaux du Haut comité consultatif de la population* ('Book no. 1 : Work of the High Consultative Committee on the Population'), PUF, 1946.

has always seemed to me a simplification of the truth, a lazy way of ignoring the richness of life.

I cannot deny, though, that in my experience harmonious unions between Russian women and French men are rare. I have even considered the latter 'the real victims of the October Revolution', if only because of their spouses' endless, bitter criticism of France, which is depressing even for a reasonably objective Frenchman. An attitude that's all the more surprising when I recall female émigrés who made brilliant, socially successful matches, bringing to the union only the memory of a more or less glorious past and sometimes, it is true, a name. If the victim (the Frenchman) felt he had married beneath himself, he was soon disabused of the idea: it was the other party that had married beneath herself, and he was made well aware of it.

One day, I happened to hear an exchange between a son and his Russian mother, who had married an extremely rich marquis from a renowned French family. Hearing his mother criticize his country yet again, he shouted, 'You're a foreigner. What are you doing here with us? Go away.' She was stunned and complained that he was being unfair.

Dozens of Russian women made brilliant marriages. I'll cite just three of them, as a matter of interest: one Russian married the great petroleum magnate Sir Henri Deterding, a second married the maharaja of Kapurthala, and the extremely wealthy aesthete Lord Abdy was so smitten with a mannequin he saw in an haute couture salon that he went on to marry her.

The majority of Russians prefer to mix among themselves. I should point out straightaway, though, that the same tendency can be observed among almost all displaced peoples. The memory of the distant homeland gnaws away at you, devours you, hurts you, so you recreate it on a tiny scale by talking, thinking and eating in Russian. You can sing the same songs together, recall the death of the same tsar, hate the Bolsheviks together, support one another with the same hopes and warm one another's hearts, chilled by the misfortune of exile.

They consider the presence of large numbers of French people an intrusion. I remember a concert Rachmaninov gave at the Théâtre des Champs-Élysées before the war, where the vast majority of the audience were his compatriots. During the interval I heard a lady exclaim in scandalized tones, 'It's unbelievable. It's full of foreigners.' The French people who had lost their way and ended up at the concert spoke their own language.

It would not take much for the Russians to cry, 'France for the Russians!' But when I suggest this slogan, they do not enjoy my joke. Teffi would have appreciated it, but Teffi is no longer with us.

*

This supposedly indolent people put extraordinary energy into recreating their little Russia in France, even before they accepted the fact that they would never return home.

Their first concern was to keep intact their children's sense of belonging to the abandoned homeland, so they set up schools, 'to fight to save their souls,' as Professor Kovalevsky writes, giving the details of all the schools in the host countries. He says that as early as 1924, there were forty-seven secondary schools in France—but I'll stop here, as I'm not writing a statistical tome. I instead refer interested readers to the author's two volumes already cited above.

Overall, the Russians got by with considerable ingenuity, all the more remarkable considering that many had never worked in their lives. What didn't they do in exile? They were mannequins, salesmen and women, officers, labourers, dish washers, painters and decorators, maîtres d'hôtel, and more. Generations transformed themselves into singers or film extras, Georgian princes became ballroom dancers, soldiers signed up to the Foreign Legion, etc. etc. As soon as General Wrangel's defeated army docked in Constantinople, it was accosted by touts looking for new recruits. Hundreds of men joined this legendary army with its romantic aura and promise of exotic countries, sun and adventure—mirages far from any desert were already forming.

Hundreds of Russians served in the regular army, and were later involved in the Resistance. The best known include Zinovy Peshkov, adopted son of Maxim Gorky, who joined the Foreign Legion and ended his career as a brigadier general. Prince Amilakhvari became a colonel and died at El Alamein leading the 13th Demi-Brigade of the Foreign Legion. Another soldier in the French army was Purishkevich, nephew of the famous lawyer and Duma deputy of the same name who was the prime mover behind the assassination of Rasputin. And not to forget Michel Garder, a French colonel of Russian birth, professor at the École de Guerre and the author of many books, including *La Guerre secrète des services spéciaux français* ('The French special services' secret war').

A whole chapter could be devoted to Russian taxi drivers, who included generals, priests, lawyers, even a doctor of philosophy and a grand duke, as we have already seen. At one time there were four thousand of them, enough to need two unions, with their own lawyers. They had garages, cooperatives, libraries, canteens, rest houses, and not only a newspaper with the inevitable title *Le chauffeur russe*, but also a magazine, appropriately named *Au volant* ('At the wheel'). The latter numbered Bunin and Kuprin among its contributors, so it must have had some literary merit. The Russian chauffeurs' balls had such a good reputation that we flocked to them, and the same can be said for their charitable evenings and their concerts. It was a small separate world with its own traditions, rules and ethics.

I knew former ladies-in-waiting transformed into restaurant waitresses or cloakroom attendants in nightclubs, who traced their origins back to the first Muscovite boyars. I still know some today who, quite shrunken with age, have been scurrying from kitchen to table for forty years, performing the same gestures, asking customers the same questions, notebook in hand.

The Russian emigration had schools, military colleges, seminaries, a conservatoire named after Sergei Rachmaninoff, which still exists today, countless churches and cathedrals, and especially that essential glue in a large human community: the press. According to V. Abdank-Kossovsky,[*] one of those who most thoroughly studied emigration at its outset, Russians published sixty-two newspapers and magazines in France—a considerable number for an émigré population of five hundred thousand souls. The same author writes that 1,005 magazines and newspapers were published in the early years of the Russian diaspora. Paris took first place in Europe with its 62 publications, but in the

---

[*] Vladimir Abdank-Kossovsky, a colonel in the imperial army's sappers, collected photographs, newspaper articles, letters and other documents about the emigration which he later sorted into chronological order under the title *La Russie impériale* ('Imperial Russia'). I found much valuable information in these texts, which his widow kindly lent me.

Far East, Harbin, with 147 titles when the White armies were concentrated there, topped that; there were 33 in Shanghai, 50 in the United States, 11 in Africa and 4 in Australia. As for books, around ten thousand were published in Russian over fifty years of emigration, Professor Abdank-Kossovsky tells us.

The churches and chapels of the émigrés are disappearing one after the other, just like the émigrés themselves. It is the same in my sixteenth arrondissement, where there had been a high concentration. I still mourn a tiny chapel situated between two gardens on Rue de la Tour, where I would go to dream more than to pray. At that time, though not a believer, I wasn't wholly ungodly, so easily is our poor human heart divided as it beats and hopes between two eternities, the one that came before and the one that may lie ahead. I spent moments of rapture there in silence and solitude, under the attentive gaze of the saints, whose gilded icons lined the little room, illuminated by the light of the sun and the Spirit.

The chapel was demolished and the trees mercilessly felled to make way for a building that taunts me with its nine ugly storeys when I happen to pass—a disastrous venture that is repeated a thousand times over in Paris.

'The form of this world passeth away', and how much more so in a great capital devoured by real estate.

It passeth slowly when history moves slowly, but if war or revolution come, it falls apart in the roar of arms. Think of the October Revolution, a cataract that swept away in its torrents of blood an empire, a tsar, the Orthodox Church, privileges, fortunes and castes. The October Revolution is a turning point in history; it is the Great Enemy of some, the Great Hope of others, but in becoming a historical term it has been emptied of its human content. Behind this abstraction disappears the individual destiny formed of blood, flesh and suffering. Fortunately, one might say, since our heart cannot bear the full view of the tragedies that the revolution wrought on the victims on all sides. And that is true of all the great historical catastrophes.

On my own very small scale, I have forgotten the suffering of my father and my sisters, and my own youthful suffering that began at dawn on the 17th of October. It too has become an abstraction, like the revolution. Our faculty for stowing away is our salvation. It allows us to slough off the past and metamorphose ourselves throughout our lives. Woe to those who do not possess this faculty and live with their eyes fixed on the past, like some émigrés who are unable to tear their gaze away. My father was one of them—he knew this pain until the last days of his life, which is without doubt a sort of psychological illness.

Let us change tone (which is frowned upon in literature) and plunge into a particular clan of émigrés, the one that by rights I belonged to: the Caucasians. They were numerous, and many were part of a sub-clan, one might say, that of the former oil barons. Some had come, like my family, with jewellery that they sold 'while waiting for the Bolsheviks to go', which allowed them to live like moguls before plunging into poverty or dying in beauty.

The particular situation of one of our great oil families excited broad interest. The head of the family had been the first in the clan to leave the Caucasus, when it was still independent. Though he had no children of his own, he had, perhaps in compensation, an astonishing number of nephews: twenty-five, it was said. They had all put their trust in him, giving him power of attorney to sell some of their oil wells, which were very soon to be nationalized by the Bolsheviks. Having an inkling this might happen, the uncle sold the wells one after the other to Western optimists who were also convinced that the 'usurpers' would soon be removed. He soon found himself in charge of a large fortune that he cheerfully set about spending. He had such a mania for luxury that he ordered a Rolls Royce with gold accessories and bought racehorses. For the Rolls Royce and racecourse he required a mistress of great luxury: he acquired one in the form of a renowned, even celebrated, actress. So he led a pleasant life, if a touch monotonous to my mind (though my opinion is hardly relevant), until the fateful day when he saw one of his nephews arrive, who had escaped from the now wholly Soviet Caucasus. He had to give him a significant sum. Two weeks later a second came, then a third, and one after the other the twenty-five sons of his brothers and sisters, some even accompanied by wives and children, arrived in Paris.

Thus began the uncle's nightmare: his nephews were claiming their share, but he wanted to keep it, or at least a good part of it, the best part. They did not agree, he did not agree at all, and in order to avoid discussions and claims he tried to escape them—no easy task. At a pinch he could close the door to them and give instructions to his servants to persuade them not to wait for him. It was more difficult for him to escape them outside the house. They were cunning too and would station themselves outside the entrance and on street corners where he was to pass. They kept spies who informed them of their uncle's movements and the visits he was to make, and they were so well organized that the inevitable happened: at least one of the twenty-five caught him as he passed and insulted him, threatened him and even begged him. The uncle put up a bitter fight. He swore he had sold only a few, almost worthless, wells and when asked for the accounts he dodged the issue by claiming to be ill and at death's door. Sometimes he threw the dogs off the scent with prodigious skill, and would leave to restore his nerves in a spa town or two accompanied by the same celebrated actress, that indispensable attribute of his luxury life.

During this time the nephews pleaded poverty, some with good reason: the apartment of one had been sequestered twelve times, literally; the radiators of another had been sealed off by the owner for non-payment of rent which obliged the unfortunate tenant to swallow aspirin tablets to get warm. A third threatened to commit suicide and made one attempt, but prudently, so that he was rescued without too much difficulty, but nonetheless it afforded him a healthy sum of money from his repentant uncle.

If anyone mentioned work, the nephews would snort disdainfully: 'Work? Us? When that monster is lazing in his Rolls? Never.' One could not entirely blame them.

Besides, none of them had a profession. They could have gone to work for a nightclub, so that it might boast of having Caucasians, but they found the idea humiliating. They could have married rich Americans, because some of the throng of nephews were very handsome: tall, well built, with fiery looks and wasp waists, but all the rich ladies on the world market at the time had already been snapped up by Georgians, who specialized in the field and were so enterprising that they always appeared first on the scene.

Enterprising—and the most handsome of the handsome. Let us not forget that the Georgian race is considered the most handsome in all the Caucasus. Too bad if Stalin-Dzhugashvili, the most enterprising Georgian of all but in a very different field, undermines this reputation—he was not known for his appearance. Like many Caucasians, his compatriots had a smouldering look and were as svelte as poplars, and had besides a major quality that made them eminently desirable in the eyes of rich commoners: a princely title, sometimes fake, but even then they made as good an impression as a true prince and provided the same services.

'You know,' one Georgian's father said, 'I'm a prince now! Usually we inherit our titles from our parents, but I've got mine from my son.'

To seduce one of America's richest young ladies, another did not hesitate to pose as heir to the throne of Georgia, claiming that he could enter only a morganatic union. He sighed at the thought of the lost throne, moving the heart of the young Yankee who collapsed in his arms. He welcomed her as a gallant gentleman would. An abdication was performed and the fiancée concluded that her seduction had outweighed the kingdom of Georgia. She did not know that the Russians had colonized it over a hundred years ago, but she did know that the Bolsheviks reigned there, and had begun to hope like all the White émigrés that 'they'll go soon'. The organizers of the renunciation of the throne gained substantial benefits through the intervention of the dethroned fiancé, and they all parted on the best of terms. Prince and Princess X flew off to a dazzling destiny, which ended a few years later in divorce, also dazzling, but nonetheless profitable for the deposed husband.

The Armenians are among the most resourceful of the Caucasians. Their business sense and keen intelligence are known throughout the orient, winning both respect and envy, often at the same time. Many go into business in France, from the small grocery store to international commerce, taking in mechanics' workshops on the way. Many prosper. An often cruelly persecuted minority in many eastern countries, they perhaps suffer less than other émigrés from displacement.

It should be noted that in Azerbaijan, with its overwhelmingly Muslim population, they at least had the advantage of the massacres not being all one way, without the opportunity for vengeance, as in Turkey. They took their revenge in Baku under the noses of our Russian masters, who saw no problem in these outbreaks of Islamo-Christian hatred and let them take their course without intervening. In 1905, at the time of the first aborted Russian revolution, the Armenians massacred us in response to a previous massacre they had suffered. Likewise, severely massacred by us at the time of the Turkish occupation of Azerbaijan at the end of the 1914–18 war, they did the same to us after the enforced departure of the ephemeral Ottoman occupiers. Which obliged us to flee to Persia, under conditions that in retrospect could be considered romantic. We boarded an oil tanker belonging to the family firm, my father disguised as a stoker, unrecognizable in all the coal dust; we women and girls, veiled from head to toe as good Muslims should be, played the family of the brave captain who was risking his life to save us.

After this brief historical overview of the fate of Armenians in Azerbaijan, let us return to their fate as émigrés in France.

One of them had a fabulous stroke of luck, independent of his merits, as all luck is. He too was an oil baron from Baku and just before the war in 1914 had ordered boats which could never be delivered to him, and were used instead to transport goods (or arms?) throughout the hostilities, which meant that on his arrival in France he found a large fortune waiting for him on a gold salver and had only to take it. He became infatuated with a very young woman whom he made first his mistress, then his adopted daughter, but finished by disinheriting her. He was considered pitiless. It can be said of him that he was very rich and very much hated, and died very old. For an émigré he had a highly envied and highly enviable fate.

At the thought that the same thing could have happened to my father, I feel certain it is an illusion to believe oneself the master of one's fate: circumstances are more powerful than the most powerful will. I also feel regret, for myself, of course, who had so much trouble making ends meet, but more for my father and some members of my family, who died in poverty if not destitution. But as he would have said with his visceral fatalism, 'This is the will of Allah.' We would so often like to substitute our will for his—let's move on.

We should mention in passing another Russian Armenian, who achieved resounding success in France in an entirely different field from boats and fortunate interruptions in delivery—that of literature, in which he was honoured by the Academy. I'm talking about Henri Troyat, who had an Armenian father and Russian mother.

French literature has an abundance of writers whose origins lie in the post-revolutionary emigration. We could draw up an impressive list. As for what will remain of them, that is a question no one can answer but is secondary, after all, to my mind at least. These writers interest me only as émigrés.

If the reader has been kind enough to follow me thus far, he will have noticed my continued emphasis on the differences that separate us from the Russians, us Caucasians of the north, south, east and west, and us Azerbaijanis in particular. Though we were taken away from Persia by the Russian conquest, we did not lose our race, which clearly has nothing Slav about it, or our religion or our language.

The assimilation of colonized peoples, which is the dream of any normal colonizer, was not easy in ethnically different countries, especially those devoted to Islam, an Islam often uncompromising and fanatical. My grandmother, for example, who did not even speak the language of the Russians, hated them with a passion; were they not offering us, imposing on us, a civilization that threatened to destroy our beliefs, our traditions, our integrity by means impossible to imagine—mixed marriages, and also by the simple attraction of dangerous freedoms? She expressed her revulsion and distrust in primitive style by spitting at the sight of giaours, the impure.

Certainly already contaminated by this civilization that assailed us on all sides, I did not hate the Russians, but I felt myself deeply other, so I was and still am shocked when I'm lumped together with them. When anyone says to me, 'you Russians', my non-Slav heart skips a beat.

I feel so distinct from them, the Russians over there and the Russians over here, with their nationalism, not to say chauvinism; their need to cling with their whole émigré outlook to a dead past. Something else immense also distinguishes them from me, perhaps to my discredit: a love of their homeland, a love I have never known, because Russia is nothing to me, and the Caucasus very little, a place where I was born but where I never felt at ease for reasons that my reason doesn't know.

And for other reasons that my reason doesn't know either, I feel at ease in the West without denying my part of the East, which I feel is alive in the depths of my being. In this regard too, everything separates me from the Russians who seem to me to be located halfway between East and West, so specifically themselves and nothing else.

That's enough on this subject.

*

Before closing this chapter, where I've been able to give only a sketchy idea of this emigration, historically unique in terms of its importance and deserving of a doctoral thesis at the Sorbonne, I will reproduce the greetings that I happened to read, and I hardly ever read newspapers, in *Russkaya mysl* ('Russian thought') on the 31st of December 1970.

So, a little over half a century since these émigrés entered the history of the West, there were still military bodies in France which sent and received Christmas and New Year greetings. I imagine that their members were mostly old men who over these fifty years had not lost their keen sense of belonging to what still represented the reason for their passage on this earth. You may draw your own conclusions:

The Central Management of the Union of Russian Disabled Veterans in France

Conveys its greetings... etc. Signed: the president of the union, Colonel Kireyev, and the secretary general, Cornet Valuyev.

The Union of Cossacks

Brother Cossacks, the year 1971 is arriving... (a long text follows on the sickness that has afflicted their homeland,

Russia, ending on the hope that a liberation movement will become established and truth will triumph). Signed: President Kuznetsov, Secretary Lomakin.

The Pyramid of the Don

(A long text follows in a similar vein to the preceding one and ends with the greeting: 'Let us forget, men of the Don, our disagreements and undertake to affirm Cossack unity.') Signed: Yeronin, Captain of the Cossacks.

The Union of Veterans in France of General Kornilov's First Kuban Campaign

We congratulate with all our hearts our companions in arms… etc. Signed: President of the Union of the Capitoline Yelatich.

Dear Companions of Alexev,

I congratulate you, your families, the Honoured Members and the Committee of the Women's Association. (A text that ends with the hope that the New Year will see their homeland liberated.) Signed: the president, Lieutenant-Colonel Kobylinsky.

The Leadership of the Russian Section of the UNO

The greetings are signed by President Drozdovsky and Secretary General Kolomytsev.

The Society of Grenadiers Abroad

The greetings are signed by the president, Lieutenant-Colonel Volkov.

The President of the Committee for the Defence of the Russian Orthodox Church Against Communism in West Germany

Greetings follow, signed by President Alimov, Vice-President Milov and Secretary Kravchenko.

Count Arakcheyev's Nizhny Novgorod Cadet Corps

The greetings are signed by President Zmetnov.

The German Union of Graduates of the Cadet Corps in Russia and Abroad

The greetings are signed by Honorary President Shpakovich.

The General Union of Cadets in France

The greetings are signed by President Gering.

The Third Moscow Cadet Corps of Emperor Alexander II

The greetings are signed by Shpilevsky.

These are followed by *The Union of Cossack Combatants, The Union of Artillerymen of the Don, The Combatants in the Kuban and Drozdov Campaigns, The Committee of the Union of Institutes, The Members of the Alexandrov Military School, The Members of the Union of Air Pilots, The Emperor Alexander III's Third Regiment of the Hussars of Pavlograd Station.*

Has this list convinced the reader of the extraordinary vitality of all these unions, all these committees, all these corps of this and that, which have come down to us fifty years later?

To finish, let us outline some aspects of the émigré attitude during the German occupation of France. As in any group of people, especially one of this size, there is black, white and grey.

The grey attitude: this is neutral. It is certainly the most frequent, because it best suits the average man. One tries to escape enormous historical pressures by remaining on the margins of events. At the heart of a menacing situation one tries to protect what one can by prudence and cowardice, or through a quite common natural disinterest in what happens beyond the confines of the small life, the small personal interest.

The white attitude: this tends towards heroism. Many émigrés rallied around the Resistance because their suddenly awakened patriotism transcended their political opinions. Russia threatened with annihilation became their Russia again, which they had to defend even on foreign soil. A smaller number of White Russians certainly felt solidarity with defeated France, and as French patriots resisted the Germans. These did not return to the USSR, as the Soviets invited all émigrés to do. Others did return, but only a small number of them, and some went back to France.

The black attitude: these were the collaborators, who were divided into two groups. Some collaborated for ideological reasons, seizing the unexpected chance to liberate their Russia of past times from the Bolshevik yoke. We remember in particular Vlasov's army.

Others became collaborators out of a desire to get rich. They served the German army as intermediaries, supplying materiel that they looked for wherever it could still be found. They amassed large fortunes in this way.

Another, more modest, category worked to survive as interpreters, while others, more shamefully, became informers.

Like all the occupied always and everywhere, every Russian reacted according to temperament, ideology or, more passively, personal circumstance.

The Great Parisian Future

Let's get back to Gulnar. We're not really leaving the White emigration, at least not yet, as the party she gave at the Josézous's brought into her life Nikolai Karpov, a true White émigré, as well as Michel Murat's acquaintance Jérôme de Labusserie, a true Frenchman from the best of circles.

It's impossible to imagine two more different people. All they had in common was their male gender. Nikolai Karpov was quintessentially Russian; handsome, stupid, uncultured, desirable and had a wonderful physique—while Jérôme de L. was fragile, 100% French, from old provincial stock, and wonderfully free of prejudice, be it national or of any other kind; his mind was open to the winds and storms but refused to be carried away by them, whether out of philosophical considerations or purely physical ones—that is, poor health. Civilized down to the soles of his feet, which were 'too small for a man' (according to contemptuous Nikolai), cultured and cosmopolitan, he yearned to transform Gulnar into an accomplished woman.

While Nikolai was to perform the functions of a stand-in lover for several months, Jérôme was to become a long-term teacher; patient, tactful, handling the unpolished Gulnar with discreet dexterity, teaching her a thousand things without appearing to do so, in a subtle but penetrating game.

Once more, Gulnar found herself blessed by fortune, which had placed on her bumpy, rutted road the man that she most needed, unbeknown to her, who was going to polish a rough diamond until all its facets shone.

I was consumed with jealousy. I realized that thanks to Jérôme she would become wittier, more attractive, more striking by the day. Already an object of desire, she would become even more desirable, and to men who were harder to conquer. Alongside her, I would have no hope of attracting anyone. This feeling of inferiority eventually extinguished me. I was already Cinderella in the most complete, the most etymological sense of the name. I represented ash and Gulnar fire. She even attracted men who did not desire her as a woman, as Jérôme's attitude shows. He was certainly kind to me but he felt a particular ardour for Gulnar, a desire to protect, a desire to make her perfect. She was his Galatea, he was her Pygmalion, though never going beyond the bounds of being her teacher. Why? Was he homosexual, or impotent?

No one had known him to have the least liaison, not even a vaguely sexual attachment (according to Michel Murat). In this regard Jérôme would always remain an enigma to us. This singular character had gained three doctorates: in law, literature and comparative linguistics, though he wasn't using a single one of them. There was no question that he was rich, though he avoided all cheap ostentation and lived very simply. On this subject too, Michel Murat provided valuable information. The studious Jérôme had received not one, but two inheritances, and was quite astonished to find himself in possession of a considerable fortune, which he did not really need since his own already allowed him to enjoy fine travel and a life devoted to culture. Why would he work for money, taking jobs that others needed urgently? He was planning to write a scholarly book about the relationship between the cursed poets of the nineteenth century and industrial society at its height, and this project kept him glued to the chairs of the Bibliothèque nationale for entire days. He spent the rest of the time travelling, frequenting the cafes of Saint-Germain, and receiving the intellectual elite in his apartment on the boulevard of the same name, where the furniture and rare artefacts created an ascetic and refined atmosphere.

His infatuation with Gulnar inspired in him something of a passion for proselytism, a desire to connect her to his own culture and awaken in her a taste for it. You had to hear him reciting Racine to Gulnar, who was bored rigid and not even bothering to hide it. But Jérôme persevered, convinced that through patience he would make her appreciate the beauty of the verses he was serving her as a fine delicacy:

> My father's sire was king of all the gods;
> My ancestors fill all the universe.
> Where can I hide? In the dark realms of Pluto?*

---

* Racine, *Phaedra*, Act IV, Scene 6, trans. by Robert Bruce Boswell, The Harvard Classics, Vol. 26, Part 3, P.F. Collier & Son, New York, 1909–14. [Translator's note.]

Well, obstinacy sometimes pays. One day, when he was reciting these verses for perhaps the twentieth time, Gulnar cried
out in astonishment: 'But it's so beautiful!' The trainer gave
a great sigh of satisfaction, smiled beatifically and kissed the
hand of the domesticated donkey. This first triumph renewed
his resolve to pursue his experiment—yes, it did indeed feel
like an experiment.

'The day you learn to love Racine, the dome of the Val-de-
Grâce and Camembert is the day you will understand French
civilization,' he said to Gulnar.

'But really, what for?' she asked, leaving Jérôme speech-
less. Recovering his spirits, he gave the only answer that could
convince my dear cousin:

'To enhance your beauty.' He was clearly thinking about
intangible beauty, but did not want to go too far down this road,
as the other was better suited to Gulnar—abstraction was not
her forte.

'Dear Gulnar,' Jérôme resumed a few moments later, 'last
night I had a strange dream that I hope is prescient.' Seeing our
quizzical glances, he explained in professorial tones, 'That is to
say, gives notice of something that is to happen. I saw you as
the reincarnation of Mademoiselle Aïssé. This daughter of a
Circassian chieftain, and so a cousin of both of yours in some
respects, was kidnapped at the age of four by the Turks, who
were pillaging her father's palace, and then sold in Constantinople
to the ambassador of France, the Count of Ferriol. He sent or
took her—I no longer know—to France where she was raised
by Ferriol's sister-in-law alongside her own son, d'Argental.
With every passing year she became more beautiful, cultured
and charming, not forgetting her romantic fate and oriental air.

She became the darling of Paris and her renown reached the ears of the regent, Philippe of Orléans, who wanted to meet her, and once he had, wanted to make her his mistress. She had the strength of character to repulse his advances, for the regent himself had plenty of charm. True, she must have already been in love with the Chevalier d'Aydie, which makes her resistance less commendable. She and the chevalier had a great love affair and she gave birth to a daughter. Why did they not marry? I confess I've forgotten the reason. Mademoiselle Aïssé remained Mademoiselle Aïssé, but she has gone down in history for her letters to Madame Calandrini which are truly a mine of information on society at that time, in particular on Madame du Deffand and Madame de Tencin. Mademoiselle Aïssé also wrote books, which have been rather forgotten over the years. But her romantic history inspired three plays, and a book by someone named Courteault, entitled *A Seventeenth-Century Idyll*. Many are still interested in this charming figure, this oriental who wrote in polished French and had plenty of talent. She died in Paris around the 1730s. May her Circassian soul rest in peace.'

Gulnar had been listening attentively, which was unusual for her. This short story, half-Parisian, half-oriental, had caught her imagination, striking an untouched chord in her inner symphony where only a single leitmotif had featured until now: success with men. The untouched chord? The ambition to succeed in other accomplishments, much longer-lasting than perishable physical attraction: to become somebody in the Paris of arts and letters; to be read, known, admired, go down in history perhaps like the Circassian, the silly goose who as the regent's favourite could have played the role that was to be Madame de Pompadour's later. How wrong she was to have rejected his advances, Gulnar thought. 'If I had been her, I...' she declared. Alas, there was no longer a regent or king of France to seduce and the statesmen of the day, all much of a muchness, did not awaken such yearnings. But I was sure of one thing: Mademoiselle Aïssé became a model for Gulnar, giving her a new-found desire to cultivate herself. From that day forwards, she was to apply herself assiduously to Jérôme's educational endeavours. Everything happened as if his dream really had been prescient and Mademoiselle Aïssé had been reincarnated in Gulnar, instilling in her gravity and a determined self-improvement. The little fairy tale, served up in a moment of inspiration by her teacher, had worked wonders. We should not forget that my vivacious cousin's mind was only waiting to be unfurled in multi-coloured flowers like a dry firework transformed into a magnificent display through the expertise of its makers.

I was consumed by jealousy once again, but over something very different from success with men. Admittedly, Jérôme, delicacy incarnate, pretended to include me in his initiation, but he didn't fool me. I knew I was just a free supplement to the main work, a secondary player, a follower. Swallowing the sense of humiliation that ate away at me, I tried to derive some benefits from this inglorious game. I read all the books that Jérôme brought Gulnar, savouring them as though they were honey, or rather ambrosia, which is said to be ten times sweeter than honey. I followed them, work permitting, on their museum visits. I pored over the art books that Jérôme offered his pupil by the dozen with the regal generosity we had come to know. I listened attentively to him discoursing on Khmer or Mayan art, or on the baroque architecture of Vierzehnheiligen or Plaza Mayor in Salamanca.

Under his stimulus I was to become Balzacian, Stendhalian, Flaubertian and Proustian all at the same time. He even had his work cut out with our musical education, as, Chopin and Beethoven aside, we were practically ignorant.

The task he had undertaken required frequent, extensive contact. Gulnar's love life had not been interrupted, though, and found her doing battle with the crazy jealousy of Nikolai Karpov. Not that he feared Jérôme as a rival. He thought it absurd that a man with a delicate constitution, 'a miscarriage of a man', as he said contemptuously, could take a woman from him, especially one such as Gulnar. But Jérôme's daily presence annoyed him so much that he could scarcely greet him politely. Whenever Gulnar talked about his intelligence, his sophistication, his culturedness, Nikolai Karpov flew off the handle, claiming that Jérôme was an imposter. He asked in all seriousness to see his degree certificates and declared that the supposed refinement that Gulnar harped on about was merely a form of extreme decadence, a mental weakness which permitted no clarity of values, only a degrading, pervasive sense of doubt. Where had he got these ideas, which did not sit well with his infantile outlook? Wherever it may be, he wielded them with aplomb as a form of self-defence against Jérôme's ever growing influence. Another way to diminish him in the eyes of his ardent mistress was to recall Jérôme's physical frailty at every opportunity. He was exhausted by the slightest effort, sensitive to the cold, wrapped up, sickly. At least Nikolai was consoled by the certainty that Gulnar would not require of Jérôme any satisfaction other than intellectual and that the betrayal would stop dead at the bed. This consolation was nonetheless poisoned by Jérôme's superiority in other domains, and Nikolai was infuriated when he found him with Gulnar almost every evening. When Jérôme eventually went home, as he liked to go to bed early, Nikolai would rage, 'I'll kill him one day. That runt, that pseudo-male!—Why do you look so tired?' he would ask Gulnar, suspicious despite everything.

'It's not from making love, you can be sure of that. Not from that monotonous kind of pleasure one always seeks in the same place. How deadly dull, even with the different variations, which are always the same too. Jérôme at least—'

'You don't get all that bored in my arms,' Nikolai interrupted, wounded. Like so many men he believed his powers of seduction second to none and imagined that he left an everlasting impression on his mistresses, while Gulnar's impressions in that regard disappeared some ten minutes after the departure of her lover.

But another object of jealousy was ravaging Nikolai, turning his life into constant torture; this time a worthy one: Otto, absent, far away but always present in his sometimes daily letters and all the material goods that came from him and were almost as necessary to Gulnar as air to her lungs.

'That dirty German,' he fumed. 'He's bound to be Jewish as well.' Like the vast majority of Russians, he sniffed a Jew wherever there was the least deviation from an indubitably Orthodox and Slav identity. When Gulnar pointed out that Otto's mother was a Golitsin, he replied not unreasonably that anyone can say anything in the absence of proof.

He resented Otto's doing business 'with those bastards' (i.e. the Soviets) and making money from them—though Nikolai himself profited too, spurning neither the caviar nor the fine wine that Gulnar served him.

'Served him'—this was through Clémentine as intermediary, who ogled Nikolai with a knowing, sardonic gaze, and was visibly delighted at the idea of the 'old man' who was being shamelessly deceived; the poor 'old man' whose letters full of love lay everywhere, and which Gulnar often didn't read to the end.

'He gets on my nerves with his love,' she said when I reproached her. 'People who impose it on you at every turn make me think of farmers who force-feed geese. You don't want any? Too bad, get it down you anyway. By the way, what an abhorrent practice. It's curious, the extent to which even the most civilized people remain brutes when it comes to pleasing their stomach. Put yourself in the place of a goose. It's true that—'

I guessed her line of thought. I didn't even have to put myself in the place of a goose, since I already was one. This was because I didn't take a lover, a topic of conversation between us whose endless repetition wore me out.

'It's true you are a goose yourself,' Gulnar continued, confirming my insight. 'An unattached young woman should normally have a lover, and if you think you're virtuous, stewing in your chastity, you can think again. You're a fool, that's all. If you really have to stand out, find another way. Besides, your virtue is an insult to me.'

'?'

'Yes, you're taunting me, behaving like that.'

'?'

'Yes, my dear, you're taunting me! How does it make me look? It's becoming intolerable. You'll do me the honour of leaving your imaginary convent where you've locked yourself up with your dreams. Oh, I know, you're waiting for the Great Love, that trap for starry-eyed girls, that mirage for the retarded mind which only really exists in penny dreadfuls.'

'Penny dreadfuls? In *The Black and the Red*, *The Charterhouse of Parma*—'

She interrupted me with this at least original retort: 'Stendhal relied on them to attract and seduce female audiences. You'd do better to look at Choderlos de Laclos...'

Jérôme would have laughed with delight to hear his pupils go at it hammer and tongs with the names of writers to whom he'd introduced them just a few months ago. We were becoming presentable, thanks to the thin coating of polish he had given us. Mademoiselle Aïssé was beginning to take on solid form.

'It's gone on long enough. I thought Jérôme could find you a lover among his many relatives, and he's already looking.'

Finding the strength to fight back against this humiliating enterprise, I cried angrily, 'I'm not a cat looking for a tom. I don't want a man that I haven't chosen myself. Once is enough.' I was referring to my unfortunate marriage. 'After all, I've got the right to be what I am. Jérôme, yes, Jérôme himself, once said that not everyone can be a libertine. I'm not made for libertinage after all.'

Neither Gulnar nor Jérôme paid any heed to my words, which vanished in the wind. No more than a few days after this conversation my cousin made an announcement: Jérôme had found me a suitor.

'He's his cousin by marriage to a cousin by marriage. He lives in Orléans. He's a surgeon, widowed, gentle, rich, a soul in search of a mate. Not at all the kind of libertine you seem so afraid of for some obscure reason. Jérôme piqued his interest the other day and he's dying to meet you. Apparently, he's not overly clever or overly cultured but very very kind and you can make of him what you will.'

'I don't want anything to do with him. You can keep your not overly clever, not overly cultured gentleman—just right for me, as I understand it, a not overly clever reject.'

'You're so stupid! He'll be your test run, precisely because he's so amenable. You'll sharpen your claws on him.'

Gulnar certainly had a way with words! Again a picture of a cat and its tom flashed before me.

'I really don't want your amenable surgeon.'

Gulnar seemed not to hear me. 'He's coming here tomorrow evening with Jérôme and the four of us are going out for dinner. It will be lovely.'

'For whom?' I yelped, rather than said.

'For all of us,' Gulnar replied with Olympian serenity.

I didn't sleep all night. I both desired and deplored this meeting which seemed obscene to me, since the four of us knew where it was headed. A betrothal in all but name, a hypocritical complicity, with me at the centre showing off my charms which, after all, might not obtain the desired approval—and why should they? Burning with shame at the thought, I buried my face in the feathers of my pillow and swore to get out of the encounter.

I spent the whole of the next day like a sleepwalker, taking off and putting back on the dresses and suits in the collection like an automaton, not hearing what people were saying around me, failing to answer questions.

'What's up with you?' asked Mary, always first to notice anything out of the ordinary.

I blamed a headache, careful not to reveal the reason for my troubled state.

I returned home, torn between acceptance and rejection, between fear of refusing a gift of fate and fear of such an uncertain encounter. Gulnar herself opened the door to me, gave me a searching look and told me to go and put on more make-up.

'I'm wearing enough make-up as it is.'

'No, you're not. You have to impress this Lucien Grandot. He's a provincial. He's expecting to meet a dolled-up, brazen mannequin. You have to give him his money's worth.'

'What money's worth?' I was cantankerous all of a sudden, shocked at Gulnar treating me like a slave.

'Do you imagine I'm going to be a kept woman like you?'

She turned white with rage. 'That's the thanks I get for my concern!'

'Concern, concern! What else?' I cried, exasperated. 'I've no desire to take this provincial surgeon as a lover. Aren't I free, after all?'

'Very well, my dear. I'll simply tell these gentlemen that you're not well and cannot join us for dinner.'

She strode away with a majestic air while I regained my room, quite beside myself. Now that I could avoid it, this encounter offered all the attractions of the unknown and I was plunged into agonies of indecision once again. I heard Gulnar busying herself in the bathroom that separated our two bedrooms. I imagined her preparations, a lump in my throat. Jérôme and the Candidate were to come for us at around eight o'clock, and as every passing minute brought their arrival closer, my desire to meet the stranger grew. But if Gulnar did not come to ensnare me once again, how would I get out of the embarrassing situation I had so foolishly got into?

Agitated, I strained my ears, hoping she would come to see me, but no, she had finished fussing around the bathroom and had gone elsewhere. The front doorbell rang. I heard voices in the distance, laughter, the promise of a party that I would be excluded from, a happiness I had refused. No one came to look for me. They left me to my Cinderella fate. No fairy godmother was going to turn me into a princess. I had been rejected, forgotten, scorned. Then, throwing my self-respect to the winds, I darted into the corridor, where I could hear Gulnar coming. I caught her passing and cried in a voice trembling with humiliation, annoyance, desire and rancour that I had reconsidered and was going to join them.

She heard me out and was as unrestrained in victory as always. Calling me a stupid, fickle, feckless child, she rounded it off with, 'Go on, hurry up and try not to behave like a peasant. This Lucien Grandot is very nice.'

I rushed to the mirror to comb my hair and top up the rouge on my already scarlet cheeks. Embarrassed from head to foot by this body, which suddenly seemed like an object to be placed in a shop window, I went to the drawing room door but did not dare open it. I was paralysed by shyness, a sense of my own inadequacy rarely absent from my mind at that time in my life, and especially by a keen sense of shame. Every time I reached for the door handle, a reflex stronger than all my resolve stopped it, drew it back, a torment that would have been never-ending, had it not been for Gulnar's intuition. She had guessed what was happening on the other side of the door and, throwing it open, she appeared like ineluctable destiny.

'Idiot,' she murmured, then said in louder, dulcet tones, 'Ah, here she is! Come in, my dear.'

Left with no choice I walked into the drawing room, held my hand out to Jérôme and the suitor in turn, and sat on the edge of a chair, its wood sticking into my thigh, though I paid no attention. I was incapable of speech, but this hardly mattered as Gulnar was speaking for ten. Casting a furtive glance at my prospective lover, I had to admit that he had a rather attractive face and a rather elegant bearing, though I would have preferred to find him hideous in order to cut short the possible continuation of events. I was already irritated by his way of speaking, of whispering in a soft voice, by his humble look and by his lack of virility, which I was used to in a friend like Jérôme but might be problematic in a lover.

*

The first question he asked me was something a Frenchman never fails to ask a foreigner, and which is aggressively stupid, because it seeks, no, demands, a positive answer.

'Do you like France?'

Out of politeness, and even if he hates France, the foreigner has to exclaim that he adores it, hence the erroneous belief of the Frenchman that his country is universally loved. But, as I've said, Grandot was already irritating me and instead of crying with enthusiasm that I adored his country, which was true, I replied with a gruff 'yes'. In reality I was jubilant, as Grandot did not intimidate me in the least. Better still, I knew our roles were reversed; that it was I who would intimidate him and that I might make him my victim. This initial contact was enough to free me of my shyness and to make me the leader in the likely game to come.

Undaunted by my attitude, he asked another question. With her brilliant sense of timing, Gulnar jumped in to hold forth at length on my reserve and 'unsociability'.

'She's been in Paris for years but you'd think she's just escaped from the harem. So pay no attention to her surly manner. She's just shy. It's curious, though: I started to feel Parisian almost as soon as I arrived here.'

She didn't miss a chance to enhance her standing at my expense. I looked daggers at her, but she didn't deign to notice.

*

It was time to leave for dinner. Jérôme's car was waiting for us in the street. Gulnar sat next to him, forcing me to sit in the back with Lucien Grandot, who made the most of this intimacy to make a nauseating declaration: 'If you only knew how moved I am to meet a little oriental like you! Jérôme described you to me, but I must confess that the reality far exceeds my hopes. Ah, the orient!' he sighed. 'Pierre Loti, the Bosphorus, the geisha…'

'The geisha are Japanese.'

'It doesn't matter: the geisha, the disenchanted, it all evokes such delicious images. Cypresses, the Golden Horn, belly dancing…' Lyricism was gushing from his lips. Then, suddenly, he changed from emotion to a very matter-of-fact tone.

'Who is your God, exactly?'

'Oh, he's a very good gentleman,' I said, offhand.

'What did you say?' Without waiting for a reply, thirsting for knowledge, he said: 'Jérôme told me you're Muslim. Do you speak Muslim?'

'I don't know that language. My mother tongue is Azeri.'

'Azeri?' Lucien Grandot must have thought the language was related to the azure heavens, and chuckled in admiration. 'Oh, that's wonderful!'

Unable to restrain his excitement, so great it needed to find expression in a concrete gesture, he grabbed my hand, which I abruptly withdrew. My beloved was stricken.

'Don't be angry,' he begged me in his honeyed tones. 'I wouldn't make you angry for anything in the world, my little Muslim. Oh, how I would have loved to see you in your harem. Did you wear long baggy trousers? Were they transparent?'

There was no limit to his impudent imagination, and I didn't even try to enlighten him. It was enough to despise him in silence. For the rest of the journey he sighed a great deal, and ventured to talk about himself, his clinic in Orléans, his property in the Sologne which he hoped I would one day give him the pleasure and honour of visiting. I gave non-committal grunts in response and, hunched in my corner, was less welcoming than a stone statue.

Grandot's banality nauseated me, and his softness displeased me, so inappropriate in a first lover that I was resolved to reject him.

I was reckoning without my weakness, Gulnar's strength and Grandot's perseverance. He came every weekend with the sole intent of seducing me, was humbler and gentler every time, his gaze dripping honey when it rested on my person. Under the influence of thwarted love, his banality worsened, aspiring to grandeur. He sent me letters calligraphed in a neat, regular hand, which began with 'Yours eternally!' (He never forgot the exclamation mark which lent drama to his decisive words.) He brought me roses, adding that I was the most beautiful one in the bouquet; he spoke of my gazelle's eyes and my pearl teeth. Perfect in his genre, he never used, even inadvertently, an original idea, maintaining thereby an easy consistency of character with no disconcerting surprises.

Gulnar waged a relentless war against me, overwhelming me with her sarcasm and reproaches, claiming Grandot was seductive and charming, that any woman healthy in mind and body could not fail to love him. I stood firm for a whole month, then felt myself softening, so much so that one evening, in the half-darkness of the car where we were without fail relegated to the back seat, Grandot succeeded in taking my hand and holding on to it. I knew then that I was lost.

Should I recount the event that to my mind seemed like a cosmic upheaval, or keep quiet about it to avoid showing myself in the most ridiculous light? I'm raising a rhetorical question that I could have omitted, since we already know the reply.

It began with a tête-à-tête dinner with Grandot, something that had never happened before, as I would go out with him only in a foursome. In times of plenty, when food is abundant, a man who has his sights on a woman feeds her up before consuming her himself. He force-feeds the victim before leading her to the sacrificial altar; he oils and fattens her, flambés her with alcohol, warms her up in every way possible. Let's not pity her too much: she submits eagerly to these preparations, even if she adopts a submissive expression for decency's sake. In this arachnoid feast, two spiders clash, and no one can predict who will devour whom.

Blessed in those days with the appetite of a Mongol horseman, I had no trouble in consuming a medium-sized chicken beneath Grandot's tender gaze, washing it down with numerous glasses. I felt I had the soul of an ogress. I was an ogress resolved to give in to Grandot's advances, but at the same time to keep the upper hand over this man who inspired my contempt but scarcely my desire. I was free and intended to remain so to the end of days, and in order to prove it to myself I ordered another glass of cognac beneath the tender gaze of my future lover, who remained undaunted by my navvy's appetite and my haughty attitude. The effects of the alcohol were softening my warrior mood and I surrendered my hand to Grandot, who twisted it in an excess of juvenile passion, despite his forty years, a detail I've omitted to mention.

After dinner he took me to the Bois de Boulogne, where he made sure to stop the car in a deserted avenue to show me the moon perched stupidly on the treetops, ready, he said, to illuminate our romantic encounter. He sighed, called me his 'cruel little geisha' and tickled my neck with his kisses, playing the transfixed lover—unless he really was. During this time a split occurred within me which was to remain constant throughout our relationship: his platitudes disgusted me, filled me with contempt, but my flesh trembled at the touch of his lips. And the Bois was full of a tender beauty, after all, the world was smiling at me through its sky and trees; it held treasures within reach—I just had to stretch out my hand. I abandoned myself to the great illusion, which was to be short-lived.

Now the car was driving beneath the canopy of a garage on the Rue Bergère. Pastoral Street—what a pretty name, and how misleading! Hardly pastoral at all. I entered the hotel where Grandot always stayed. I seethed with resentment because he obliged me to walk past the perceptive gaze of the concierge, who already recognized what I wanted to ignore—the first step in my downfall. Then I had to get into the lift in close intimacy with Grandot, a stranger to me, beneath the mocking gaze of the young lift attendant, who also knew what my immediate future would be—the second step in my downfall. And the numbered door to the room opened to the ignominious sight of a large bed, where I was to do my apprenticeship in that longed-for freedom. I was angry with Grandot for failing to spirit away these steps, each more humiliating than the last, which completed my downfall.

I sat in a chair without taking off my hat and coat, gripped by shame and hatred, resolved to make him pay for these humiliations by humiliating him myself. Brimming with hope, he perched uncomfortably on the arm of the chair and started kissing me in all the places where the leading men in films kiss their leading ladies, kisses I had wanted so much. But my mind revolted, my body followed, and I pushed Grandot away. He had to hang on to the back of the chair to stop himself falling off. 'Leave me alone. I'm going,' I shouted hoarsely.

'My dear, you can't. You can't do that to me! I love you.'

I was indignant to hear such vulgar language.

'Ha ha!' I gave what I hoped was a satanic laugh, to make clear my contempt, my distaste and my doubts about this love.

Grandot would have been amazed to learn what contrary winds were buffeting my mind. Because I wanted love, even the love of this man whom I despised. I aspired to love, ready to apply it to any object, because I was young, because 'my heart was yearning', to use Stendhal's phrase; because my body too was screaming its thirst as desire throbbed. But I panicked at the idea of getting undressed in front of this stranger, of getting into bed to submit to the contact of foreign flesh. I was starting to miss my husband: I had never found him physically attractive, but at least, once all the mortifying preliminaries had been completed, I had stopped feeling overwhelmed by modesty when intimate with him. Habit and time, which render everything banal, had done their work. But let us return to poor Lucien Grandot, whose face reflected the extent of his disappointment, which only spurred my fury.

'Why do you have to bother me?' I flung this question in his face like a poison arrow.

He plunged into a sea of lamentation, spoke of his tenderness and my cruelty and wrung his hands, which were long and fine, worthy of his profession; he even went as far as pretending to tear out the few greying hairs he still had. The more he humiliated himself before me, the more I loathed him, because he was too obtuse to understand that his attitude left me in charge of operations, forced me to take actions that I found repellent. He should have been rough with me, forced me to submit through some imperious method, raped me if necessary, instead of distorting the game by crawling at my feet. What did he want? For me to take off my shoes, take off my clothes, get into bed in front of him, all as though it were the most ordinary thing in the world?

Before my closed, hateful face, Grandot lost the last vestiges of assurance and stammered words that I was no longer listening to, paying attention only to the rage tearing through my heart.

His complaints exasperated me. If anyone should be pitied, it was me for having fallen into the hands of this pitiful weakling. When he sat down again on the arm of my chair to try a new approach, I pushed him away so vigorously that he again nearly fell off, just managing to keep his balance.

'Leave me alone! Go to bed and give me some peace. I'm going to sleep here in this chair.'

Then Grandot wept. Yes, wept. It was appalling. Like a child, with choking sobs and tears, and between two hiccoughs he managed to stutter, 'Cruel woman, cruel,' forgetting at a stroke the 'little geisha'. My heart of steel felt not a shred of compassion in the face of this ridiculous performance. To escape it I looked blackly at the roses in the carpet beneath my feet. They were large red roses, grouped in bouquets, and carried me thousands of leagues away towards the Persia of poets, where we had sought refuge from the umpteenth historic upheaval in our native Azerbaijan. They carried me away to vast fields of roses, stretching to a distant river almost as far as the eye could see. They gave off an intense fragrance that perfumed even our dresses. A Persian sojourn that began in an idyll of peace regained but ended in a malarial fever that ravaged us one after the other. Memories in which the good and the bad were interwoven as in these garlands at my feet, memories that for a few moments made me forget the Rue Bergère in the tenth arrondissement of Paris and the surgeon seeking my love.

When I returned to him, he was pulling himself together for want of anything better to do: wiping his eyes, blowing his nose, looking at me with a meek, resigned expression. He rose, went to the bathroom and soon emerged dressed in grey pyjamas with broad blue stripes, which made him look like a clown. Nothing could have been less suited to his serious, black-spectacled face than these bright pyjamas, oh so *vie Parisienne*. I turned away in contempt.

He slipped beneath the counterpane, waited a few moments, then asked, faintly: 'Aren't you coming to bed, my dear?'

'No!'

He raised his head and looked at me sadly, then let it fall back to the pillow as though exhausted, and gave a long sigh, as eloquent as ten.

'You disgust me,' I said forcefully, and, so as not to contradict my now well-established reputation for cruelty, added: 'You look like a clown.'

'Oh,' he sighed, and was silent.

There was little we could say after this definitive declaration.

A solitary night light illuminated the corner of the bed, leaving the rest of the room in shadow, darkness and silence. I remained quiet, but malice was rampaging inside me like a great Siberian storm. And like a storm it chilled and darkened my soul, turning me into a graceless creature plotting designs of ill intent. I was wavering over how to complete Grandot's humiliation: shower him with disparaging remarks, or leave without saying a word? Following an internal debate, I opted for the latter course of action, as it would be more aristocratic of me and more humiliating for Grandot. So I got up and walked firmly towards the door.

'What are you doing?'

Grandot sat bolt upright in his bed. Without replying, I put my hand on the doorknob, but did not have time to open it. He was upon me in another bound, led me towards the bed with the strength of a Goliath and shoved me between the sheets, literally, just as I was, still in my shoes and hat and my bag hanging from my arm. Then he lay down next to me and held me in his arms, wrapped like two solid ropes around my bust.

'You're mad!' I cried, as was called for in the circumstances, but oh, I felt I had been saved. At last, he was going to rape me! And the awful malice left me, as though Grandot's ardour had drawn it to him, pulling it out through all my pores. A man's chest is such a wonderful refuge! The softest pillow in the universe cannot compete with a man's shoulder, where the head rests as though in a casket. And the warmth, the miraculous human warmth, a mixture of blood and love, and that pressure of a caressing hand, and that envelopment and that bewitchment... I lost my head to it all; not enough to stop my worrying about my crushed hat, though, my shoes on my feet and my crumpled clothes. I must have transmitted my thoughts to Grandot, because he removed my hat, my bag and my shoes and unfastened my dress. I helped him, hoping he would not notice my tacit consent; I blushed as I gave in, as though it were a shameful act.

For a while, I didn't know if it was long or short, Grandot became a god, and he remained one as long as he loved me in silence. Having become its creature, I knew that love justified the harm it could do us, that it created and recreated us; that it had been at the beginning of the world and would crown the end of time.

But the pressure of the arms relaxed, and Grandot murmured, 'My little geisha.'

And the tacky god tumbled down a vertiginous slope towards the abyss of the earth, becoming a man again like millions of others, only even more ridiculous than ordinary mortals. Nothing remained of the fairy story, the celebration.

But despite everything, the long awaited event had finally been accomplished: I had a lover; I could stand up to Gulnar; I could tell my mannequin sisters of my adventure. An overwhelming event with far-reaching implications! Ascribing the same sentiments to Grandot, I was expecting to hear him wax lyrical on the subject until dawn, delirious with joy, to make love to me until first light, and I had already forgiven him all the platitudes he would be sure to utter as he clasped me against him. I pressed

myself against this already slightly familiar flesh and Grandot responded with tenderness, then suddenly he was still. And the young imbecile in love with fantasies heard such a horrible noise that everything seemed to come tumbling down around her: he had dared to snore! Not very loudly, to be honest; we could say that he was exhaling a little too heavily. But what did decibels matter? It was the blasphemy that counted. He had dared to fall asleep and snore while I was waiting for him, panting fervently…
I tore myself out of his arms. He woke up, grunted a little and muttered something indistinct. I leapt up and threw myself, clad in my chemise, into the same chair, resolved not to move all night, even if had to die of pneumonia; a martyr I was and a martyr I would remain.

'What's wrong?' the fallen god asked, awake now. I was outraged at his stupidity and boorishness.

'Boor!' I cried.

He groaned, sat up and began negotiations to make me see reason. I found him hirsute and hideous, his eyes looking at me in that vague way the short-sighted have.

'You're ugly. Anyone would have to be out of their mind to love you. Look at you!'

I continued this accusatory monologue a while longer. Bad thoughts teemed inside me like little vipers, devouring my soul, turning me into a harpy, hell-bent on spitting insults at this poor, entirely innocent man. When I had finished, having exhausted my imagination, he cried again, got back into bed and ignobly fell asleep. As for me, my hatred kept me nailed to the chair. Around three in the morning the cold crept over me, and at first I was delighted: so much the better, I would die of some illness caught through the fault of this heartless man. He would suffer for it, he too might die of it—at least I hoped so. I would laugh then too. But I remembered that I would hardly be able to laugh in my grave, and was torn with pity for my youth cut short. It was my turn to weep: I felt abandoned, destined for every bad thing through the fault of this man who was sleeping in warmth and comfort. I sobbed a little louder to wake him up, but in vain. I sobbed properly, shifting in my chair, but still in vain. Finally, with the tip of my toe I pushed an object on the corner of the table in front of me and it fell to the floor with a loud thud. Then Grandot did wake up and found himself at the heart of the drama.

'What? You're still in that chair and hardly dressed! My poor little thing, you're crazy!'

He rushed over and wrapped me in his arms. It was high time: my teeth were chattering from cold, fatigue and nerves. The devil returned to tempt me for a moment, trying to revive my malice, but weariness was stronger: yes, stronger than the devil. I resisted just a little in order to save face, but let myself be led into the bed, face sullen but soul jubilant—paradise could be neither warmer nor softer.

*

Having finally overcome the obstacles of my own making, I settled into my relationship with Grandot, my heart churning with contradictions: while he physically delighted me with hitherto unknown pleasures, I disliked him in all other respects. I was even becoming acquainted with the first signs of intellectual snobbery in which Jérôme had initiated me. I required a man to have wit, culture and an outlook that I would readily call 'Parisian'—something that is now behind me. I despised Grandot for his lack of culture, his poor taste in platitudes and even his defencelessness in his relations with me. I don't know if it was weakness, kindness or profound indifference, but I could say anything to him, put him through anything and he would invariably react with sighs and laments.

The excellence of his character proved unequalled. It had to be, in order to counterbalance the abjectness of mine, and without it our relationship could not have lasted more than a few days.

On his return to Orléans after the first night spent with me in novel and difficult circumstances for both of us, Grandot wrote me a letter in which he deployed all his resources of bad taste, and which he concluded with a request: that Jérôme, Gulnar and I should visit him in Orléans at the weekend.

'We will relax after our daily toil with our delicious little roses of the orient.'

After making cruel fun of the letter, the delicious roses of the orient accepted the invitation and Jérôme took us to Orléans via a road that in that era was almost deserted even on a Saturday afternoon. Compared to other highways in France, there was nothing picturesque about it, but I was enchanted by the flat fields with clumps of trees surrounding an old farm here and there, by the bell towers of village churches. All of these I was discovering for the first time since I'd been in France, as I had never left Paris! The meadows filled with lush grass alone came as a revelation to me, who had grown up in our desert landscape dotted with artificially irrigated oases. I compared the real and the imaginary, as though the landscape of my childhood was superimposed on that of France. Derricks replaced the church towers, stony fields the green meadows, flat-roofed houses with gardens of stunted fig trees the villages of La Beauce. Churches topped with crosses dislodged the minarets of a mosque; blonde children took the place of swarthy infants playing jacks; the arched headstones of Muslim cemeteries faded before Christian tombs. No, I was not racked by nostalgia at these recollections, quite the reverse: I felt an unalloyed happiness at having escaped this past, whose corpse I trampled on with joy. If I resuscitated it, it was only the better to throw it back into its grave, where it would eventually disintegrate into ashes. No one appreciated their displacement more than me; no one felt better than I did in 'exile', a word I can write only in quotation marks.

Orléans, which I immediately compared to Baku, seemed to me a wonderful city. It was the second one I got to know in France after Paris. Jérôme, who never missed an opportunity to instruct us, told us the history of its siege by the English and the unlikely epic of Joan who came to fight them; showed us the cathedral, the Place du Martroi, the banks of the Loire that divided the city. Erudition, as always, flowed freely from the lips of our teacher, who had the remarkable gift of educating and entertaining at the same time; he could have delighted thousands of students, had he not preferred a life with only the constraints he imposed on himself. I think that neither Gulnar nor I fully appreciated our good fortune in having all to ourselves this awakener of the mind whose rich and varied culture was accompanied by a host of other qualities—kindness, generosity, tolerance and humour.

After this hands-on history lesson, he took us to a narrow street cut off from the world where grass grew abundantly between large cobblestones, and stopped the car outside a white house surrounded by young elms. Grandot must have been looking out for us, as the porte cochère into the courtyard garden opened almost immediately and my beloved appeared, visibly moved. He was the sentimental type, everything that I hated—and he was to be made aware of it very soon, very often, very painfully.

The car drove into the courtyard, which seemed asleep, as did the house with its small paned windows and charming, friendly feel. Despite its two hundred years, it had never seen people of our race. We must have made a bizarre impression, as suddenly it seemed to give me a wink—yes, with its bullseye window.

Grandot took me by the waist, whispering 'my darling geisha' in my ear, and led us to the first floor, to a drawing room cluttered with chairs, pictures, mirrors, vases, candelabras, all gilded or silver-plated, all gleaming with false magnificence. Large bows adorned cutwork embroidery cushions; on all sides, nudes—men, women and children—contorted themselves in unnatural poses; lace doilies and artificial flowers completed the look.

'Your home is charming,' Gulnar said, and meant it. Any normal person in Baku would have liked this drawing room. Her father had built a house in an Arabic-Gothic-Renaissance style with rooms similar to this one. Jérôme had yet to shape his pupil's taste in terms of furnishings; he couldn't do everything in a few months. He must have been secretly amused at the poor taste of this third cousin once removed, and have promised himself he would complete Gulnar's cultural education. Blessed with remarkable intuition in addition to his many other qualities, he gave me surreptitious glances, guessing my thoughts.

We drank aperitifs brought by a servant, and all of a sudden it all seemed an absurd dream. What were we doing here? We were so out of place in this French province, with the scent of Islam still clinging to us despite the few years of separation from the Caucasus. In my imagination I saw my grandmother, still veiled, still living in the time of the Hegira: what would she say if she saw us here with two giaours, one of whom was my lover? A huge wave of ennui swept over me, welling up from this return to the past. It was ridiculous: shouldn't I have rejoiced at the death of a hated world? But no, stupidly I felt the desire to cry. I frowned, steeled myself and stopped listening to the fortunately very animated conversation, in which no one even invited me to take part.

We have to fight to protect our inner equilibrium from these abrupt swings in our mental state, which assault us relentlessly for no discernible reason. They can be compared to the brutal climatic changes that our body has so often to cope with, to suffer, in order to survive. These strange moods vary in frequency and in the devastation of their impact (according to our physical or psychological constitution?) and are the plague of our human condition, as they almost always descend into depression. Rarely do they bring us moments of happiness, when everything seems to bloom within us, around us, transfiguring the world into a green meadow. The most battle-hardened man, even the most robust there is, does not escape these inner metamorphoses.

For my small part, the moods consumed me slowly or swiftly, barring my access to serenity—that inner temple, where there is neither rain nor wind.—May I be forgiven this digression. It explains my behaviour a little, but I know only too well that it does not excuse it.

I listened to all three of them and hated them all: Gulnar, with the self-assurance of a girl who doesn't know failure; Grandot, dripping in sentimentality; even Jérôme, who suddenly seemed too precious to me; but more than them I hated myself; what I was and what I would never be. I wanted to escape, to bury my face in a pillow and weep until I was sated; instead of which I proceeded with the others into the dining room, which was in even worse taste than the drawing room, but where I at least found a dinner to my liking. How contradictory our behaviour is: my subdued mood took nothing away from my appetite and I ate for two without being any more amiable towards Grandot or even showing some simple gratitude. My feelings towards him were complex and were to become more so every time we met. But were they really all that complex? They could be summed up very simply: my body loved him, my mind despised him. His lack of culture, his foolishness, his sensitivity, his lack of virility other than in bed exasperated me. I soon discovered him to be narrow-minded, to lack generosity and, worse still, intelligence, a fault that he compensated for with much affection and a knowledge of love that I appreciated, especially at the start of our relationship, but eventually found monotonous. Oh, those gestures! Who would invent new ones?

Grandot excelled at bringing out the worst in me. Some people are like certain books or certain pieces of music: some awake in us angels with silken tongues, others devils that spit fire. With Grandot, I spewed huge jets of flame with a stench of sulphur. I took pleasure in hurting him, humiliating him, making him aware of all his flaws, which he might not have known about. It didn't concern me that mine were just as great: the humpback is not embarrassed by his hump when he mocks other humpbacks, which is not surprising, after all, since he does not see his own.

All this delicious food did not give me a taste for life. On the contrary, my depression grew worse; I wanted to die, less from real sadness than from a sort of weariness and ennui: Grandot bored me, Jérôme bored me. All these stories, all these words, all these undertakings that would eventually dissolve without trace. As one can see, I was preoccupied with my moods and unbearable as a result.

Dinner ended with strawberry ice cream. 'The colour of hope,' Grandot proffered, still at the height of platitude, and gave me a meaningful look.

We returned to the drawing room, where all the gilding gleamed even more triumphantly in the electric light. Had we eaten too much, drunk too much? Was my depression contagious? Either way, conversation lagged. Even the remarkably loquacious Jérôme appeared too tired to talk and a veil of sadness seemed to cover us all. Or was my imagination playing tricks on me again?

'My little geisha,' Grandot said eventually, 'you're tired. Come to bed.'

Jérôme and Gulnar went to their rooms, while I meekly followed my beloved. A few seconds later, irony revived my taste for life; I entered a bedroom full of flounces, vases, flowers: a lamp with a pink shade (the colour of hope?) cast a pink light on the pink bedspread. But the key to my entry into the holy of holies lay elsewhere: great billows of blueish smoke filled the room; they were coming from a stand where incense and myrrh burnt in my honour.

'My dear, I wanted to surprise you, so that here in this room you might feel at home, as though in the orient. But the perfume isn't strong enough.'

He took some incense paper out of a drawer and burnt sheet after sheet until the bedroom was transformed into a test labora-tory for smoke bombs or an opium den, both equally suffocating. Choking, I managed to croak, 'Open a window, I beg you.'

*

'Nikolai is already unbearable, though he pays for nothing,' Gulnar confided to Jérôme some time later. 'What would he be like if he supported me? I wouldn't be able to go out without giving him an exact reason. Oh, long live Otto! Don't you agree, Jérôme?'

'He seems very congenial, this man whom I have yet to have the honour of meeting. He has done himself only one disservice: he leaves you alone too long.'

He had left her alone for almost five months already, urgent business summoning him variously to Moscow, Berlin and elsewhere. Soviet Russia, scarcely twelve years old, exhausted, ruined by the First World War and then by another, the Civil War, perhaps more brutal still, needed all that the West could provide. She bought, rebuilt, called technicians and businessmen to come to her rescue. Wasn't Otto a businessman? Without a scrap of evidence, Nikolai claimed that Otto was a committed spy disguised as an industrialist, and he repeated it so often that he ended up sowing doubts in Gulnar's mind, though rather than bother her the idea excited her—it gave him a romantic air.

'You've taken up with a spy,' Nikolai said with disgust, with-out specifying whether Otto was working for the West, for the Secret Intelligence Service for example, or for the Bolsheviks. He would have preferred the latter, but after all, Otto seemed steeped in capitalism. So Nikolai suggested he was a double agent, finding his interests here and there, and completed his portrait of Otto as a sneak, telltale, traitor, ready to stoop to any ignominy, an image that suited Gulnar's 'husband' as much as a crinoline suits a donkey.

That he had never been her husband even according to Soviet law was confirmed as soon as she took the necessary steps to exchange her Soviet passport for a Nansen one, thus becoming a stateless person among the hundreds of thousands of Russians and other political refugees. It was obvious that with her penchant for luxury and idleness she did not belong in a country where communist ideology was endemic. She could flourish only in a system of exploitation of man by man, or as we should say in this case, exploitation of man by woman. Besides, she was attached in her own way to the man she exploited. Unfortunately, he too suffered from jealousy, and she was preparing to confront all his suspicions.

'Why are they all so jealous?' she asked Jérôme. 'As though there were not enough of us for everyone. It will be so tiring to explain to him that, like Penelope, I have rejected all suitors during his absence.'

Two parallel signs informed us that his arrival was imminent: the cheques became rarer while the letters became more frequent and tender. The closer the arrival loomed, the more Nikolai proved irascible and brutish. I had never seen a man suffer jealousy to such a degree. It pummelled him all over like an illness: he flushed, he shook from head to toe, and he sputtered insane comments from which we realized that he was preparing to kill Otto! He frightened us, and Gulnar regretted even the precarious bond she had been foolish enough to establish with him.

'Oh God, oh God, how can I rid myself of this mad elephant? Jérôme, you have to help me. You must take him in hand, especially when Otto is here, otherwise he'll do something terrible.'

Finally, one morning Gulnar received a telegram announcing Otto's arrival the next day. I heard Clémentine murmur, 'Now we'll have some fun…'

The woman was taking ever greater liberties. Party through circumstance to Gulnar's love affairs, she thought that as a result she could do anything: a natural calculation for such a low character. She stole objects and money, listened at doors and drank all the alcohol she could find. Then, nose red, hair dishevelled, bodice unbuttoned over her vast bosom, Clémentine indulged in long monologues in the kitchen. Appealing to pots and pans to bear witness as though they were a large crowd, she dreamt up tales where she always played the beautiful leading role. She complained of her undeserved loneliness, her dashed aspirations, of being misunderstood in a cruel world where Gulnar and I had an important place.

'Oh my, youth are so heartless! They don't know what it is to be alone without a good soul to support you. Oh, when they're my age, they'll realize how mean they've been to me. But it will be too late: Clémentine will be no more.'

She must have had a good cry, as we heard her blowing her nose loudly. A gurgling sound followed, and then renewed lamentations.

Such a bitter view of the world does not encourage fortitude or energy. Influenced by her mood which never changed, Clémentine spent hours doing nothing. She left the spiders in peace to spin their webs in the corners and let small piles of dust accumulate behind the beds. Gulnar was desperate to dismiss

Clémentine, but for once her assurance deserted her. She was afraid of the drunkard's response and perhaps her revenge.

When Nikolai learnt of Otto's impending arrival he blanched. 'This time you're going to send your Otto to the devil,' he told Gulnar, who blanched in turn.

'I'm not sending him anywhere. He's staying where he is—here.'

'Very well, I will remove him.'

'You're mad!' cried Gulnar, the words of outraged women the world over for millennia. At the same time she made a haughty motion of the head, imitating Mathilde de la Mole, who had been her model for more than a month. She had got into the habit of mimicking the heroines in the novels she was reading. She was unusually good at it too. Jérôme, who witnessed the scene, admired her, as did I. I can assure you that the motion of the head, the haughty air, were just right for the daughter of a peer of France.

'You're mad!' she repeated forcefully. 'What are you planning to do?'

They glared at one another. Features strained, shoulders back, coiled as though about to pounce on an adversary in the ring, Nikolai looked like a great ape, handsome but furious. Gulnar faced him, maintaining her poise as a daughter of a peer of France, and tearing him into a thousand pieces with her stare.

'Boor,' Gulnar whispered through her teeth.

'Me? A boor?' cried Nikolai. 'I'm from a far better family than you, and I'm a colonel in the imperial army.'

'We couldn't care less.'

I mention in passing that he spoke pidgin French, which I don't transcribe here, for fear of tiring the reader. While there were many Franco-Russian restaurants in Paris, there was also an original Franco-Russian language among the émigrés, which some French people even found charming, though I did not: I hated this mutilation of two languages which resulted in clownish gobbledegook.

Let's return to our scene of jealousy and hatred. Fortunately Jérôme was there, and he filled the grim silence with philosophical musings on the state of the world. Any subject would have done the job of breaking up the battle between Gulnar and Nikolai, who fell silent. He soon pulled his large fedora over his ears, which gave him a Byronic air, and got ready to leave. Jérôme got up too, after a look of entreaty from Gulnar.

'Go after him and try to talk some sense into him, I beg you,' Gulnar murmured in his ear.

She had good reason to impute the darkest of intentions to her lover, tormented by jealousy.

'Never again will I get involved with a young man,' she said to me when we were alone. 'All their strength is channelled into jealousy. As long as Jérôme doesn't leave him and keeps him on a leash.'

I thought Jérôme would find it hard to keep Nikolai on a leash but I kept my pessimism to myself. Gulnar seemed very unhappy, and after all, I said to myself, why shouldn't she be sometimes, especially since she had woven this complicated web herself?

On Saturday, when I came home at lunchtime (we still worked Saturday mornings 'in those days', when the unions seemed unable to defend the working classes well). I found Otto rejuvenated and cheerful, and he bore gifts for Gulnar and me. The contrast between his role as a shrewd businessman and his humble attentiveness towards my cousin always filled me with amazement and pity. He was angling for a look, a kindness, the slightest gesture of tenderness. But Gulnar, more and more Mathilde de la Mole, remained distant, her dignity overwhelming poor Otto. In reality, she feared a provocation by Nikolai and perhaps thought her icy attitude would provide protection in advance against the accusations that might rain down on her pretty head.

When I was alone with Otto, he asked me, 'My God, what's wrong with her? She's changed. Her tone is so strange. She scares me. Oh, I'm very much in love, but I've aged so much and am hardly worthy of her!—She must have cheated on me,' he added uncertainly, giving me an apprehensive look.

I didn't countenance telling him the truth, especially not when his manner was calling for, begging for, lies. This poor man, so stupidly in love, filled me with compassion. I was most indignant of all at the mocking glances he received from Clémentine, who was delighted at the merry dance Gulnar led the 'old man'. I found my involuntary complicity distasteful and demeaning, but could not escape it.

The next day, a Sunday, we were chatting peaceably and sipping coffee around the table, which had been cleared of the breakfast things, when the doorbell rang. Gulnar and I exchanged looks—we understood one another. We both felt the same apprehension, as we weren't expecting anyone other than the one visitor we didn't want to see. Heavy steps in the hallway already identified the impromptu guest: Nikolai appeared in a state of advanced inebriation, followed by Jérôme, visibly dismayed at his failure as a policeman. We learnt afterwards that he had been unable to prevent Nikolai's getting drunk, although he had followed him like a shadow and even made him sleep at his, Jérôme's, home.

Nikolai walked with a heavy tread, holding himself too straight. His was the suspect gait of the drunk, rigid with the effort of keeping his balance. His eyes shone and his whole person radiated defiance. Gulnar introduced him to Otto, awkwardly, quietly, as though Nikolai's name scorched her lips.

They sat down, Jérôme coughing discreetly to give himself an air of assurance, Nikolai silent and superbly disdainful, eschewing the customary polite remarks to show he had no intention of observing that nonsense. He was going to plunge right in without alleviating the drama, quite the contrary. He stared at Otto in a cavalier fashion, and under the handsome young man's cruel gaze poor Otto shifted in his chair, opened his mouth to speak then closed it again, then seemed to sag, slump, collapse inside and wait for the final blow that he sensed was coming. Without drawing it out, Nikolai declared in a strong voice, enunciating each word, 'I have come here to claim my rights to Gulnar.'

'Nikolai, I beg you. You promised me,' Jérôme interrupted, but Nikolai seemed to sweep him aside with a grand gesture of the arm.

'Yes, monsieur, I don't know if Gulnar has informed you, but I for my part like straight talk: Gulnar and I love one another and I want to marry her.'

Gulnar stood up. I guessed that beneath the thick layer of rouge covering her cheeks, her pallor matched that of the handkerchief she was holding in her hand.

'Not only do I not love you, I hate you. I've never hated anyone as much as you. Will you please leave?'

Nikolai did not bat an eyelid. Otto was pale and silent. He directed his sad, questioning gaze at Nikolai and Gulnar in turn, as though seeking a solution that was nowhere to be found. He must have felt so humiliated, not so much by Nikolai's words as by his handsome youthfulness, a victory in itself which he could never overcome. How many times he had lamented his age, which put a gulf of thirty years between him and Gulnar, made him ridiculous in his own eyes and gave him a sense of unease, because he knew that only money could fill this gulf.

'Will you leave?' repeated Gulnar de la Mole.

'You dare to deny that you love me?' Nikolai rose, and staggered (the effect of the blow she had dealt him or of his inebriation?).

'What love are you talking about? You're rambling. I'm disgusted to see you a drunk, ill-mannered muzhik. Leave, I tell you. I don't want to see you again until the next world: hell, heaven, it doesn't matter, as long as it's not on this earth. You're a disgrace.'

Nikolai staggered again and Jérôme moved towards him as though to support him. 'Come, come, my dear friend, you're not well. Let's go.'

Deathly pale, Nikolai did not react. He let Jérôme lead him, their footsteps fading in the distance, and we heard the front door close. They had gone. The curtain had fallen on this hideous scene. Hideous in every way: an ageing man who learns of his misfortune; a drunkard who behaves cruelly and boorishly; a woman who coldly rejects him in order to keep the goose that lays the golden eggs. And it wasn't over: the scene continued, but in a very different fashion. Otto wept. He wept as I had seen Grandot weep: *'Cherchez la femme.'* We knew how to tear ourselves apart, and others too—this was the law of an abominable world, where we had the fangs of wolves.

Gulnar looked at him, incredulous. She went over to him, put her arms round his shoulders and embraced him tenderly.

'Oh no, Otto, you're not going to weep because of that drunk muzhik who got it into his head that I loved him, when I was making fun of him.'

Otto wiped his eyes, kissed Gulnar's hand, which lay on his chest, and shook his head sadly. 'He's young and handsome and I'm so old—'

'I beg you, Otto, don't be so melodramatic. Don't fall into despair because of this idiot, when all we do is laugh at his stupidity. Did you really believe a word he said? I've never been his mistress. He's in love with me and imagines that I love him.'

'?'

Gulnar was plotting. I could see from her strained face and intense gaze that she was preparing an attack. And attack she did.

'Besides, why did you leave me alone for five months? Even if I did go astray,' (she had a way with words) 'what does it matter? Lovers pass but a husband remains.' (This wasn't entirely accurate in her case either, but the wording was fortuitous.) 'Oh no, Otto, face up to it. All this is of no importance at all, none at all.'

Otto seemed calmer. After a moment's reflection he asked, 'Were there many lovers during these five months?'

'Oh no, I beg you, let's not talk about this any more. I love you, Otto, only you.'

The door opened on this fine lie and Clémentine appeared with a tray, as though to clear away the coffee.

'What do you want?' Gulnar asked harshly.

'Oh, nothing, madame. I'm just clearing up.'

Base deceit was written all over her face.

'You're lying. You've come to see what's going on here. You must have had your ear to the door and your eye at the keyhole. I've had enough of your nosiness, your drinking, your stealing. I can't even keep track of it all.'

'What? What?' Clémentine turned red with rage. One dared accuse her of such villainy, her, who was so pure, so alone, so mistreated by fate?

'Madame should withdraw her remarks, or—'

'Or what? Are you threatening me now?'

What, hadn't Clémentine been eavesdropping after all? She didn't know that threats still effective half an hour ago had lost their currency—they had been devalued, definitively devalued. Gulnar was invulnerable.

Otto rose. Pointing a commanding finger towards the door, he cried in suddenly ungrammatical French, emotion taking its toll: 'Get out. Pack your bags and leave.'

Clémentine gave a heart-rending cry, then left the room, lamenting the injustice of fate.

'Voila,' said a relieved Gulnar. It was the end of Act II.

Act III should have been the suicide of Nikolai, as she claimed he was capable of any extreme. I wonder if she wanted it to happen, as the death of a desperate lover would have been a fine flower in the garland she was weaving around her pretty head. But perhaps I'm being unnecessarily spiteful and libellous. No, Nikolai did not kill himself, but died for us nonetheless, in the sense that we never had the pleasure—or displeasure—of seeing him again.

As for Otto, after this episode he changed. At first sight he seemed to be his old self, as attentive to Gulnar, as adorable with me, always ready to smile and entertain us. He was regally munificent and showered us with gifts, and begged me to leave my job, which he considered ridiculous and unworthy of me. But I often caught him gazing into the distance, such an expression of melancholy on his face with its sagging jowls that it broke my heart. I did notice the contradiction in my feelings, for while I was always ready to pity him, I never thought to pity my own victim Grandot, who deserved it as much as Otto.

One evening when I returned to the house around seven, I found him alone in the drawing room, sitting in the half-light. His voice, his slumped posture, the atmosphere around him all revealed he had been weeping. You may raise your eyebrows, but sometimes when we walk into a room we can tell if people have been laughing there or crying. I sat down next to him.

'Yes,' he said, as though replying to my unspoken question. 'I am feeling older, and you two are so young. You're like a living reproach to my coming senility. What right do I have to monopolize Gulnar? Because I'm rich? There are others younger than me who have fortunes too—she would only have to reach out her hand.'

'She loves you, Otto, I assure you. She respects you—'

'Oh no, don't bring respect into it, please! What can I do with it? I suffer when I'm near her. When I'm far away, I imagine in a sense that I'm closer to her, and with no right other than to love the memory of her. Here, she has to put up with me. Oh, it hurts so much.'

I heard the door of the apartment close. Gulnar was back.

Two days later he left us. The two of us were alone without even a domestic help. Clémentine had gone the very day of her dismissal, leaving behind a letter in which the drunkard gave free rein to her cheap eloquence and resentment. She ended the missive with these noble words: 'I share your grief. Your misunderstood Clémentine.' We never understood why she deigned to share our non-existent grief. Instead of mourning, we were happy to be rid of her exceptionally unpleasant presence and astonished that we had put up with her for so long. Besides, fortune smiled on us: a few days later we found Marie, a delightful young woman, clean, cheerful, kind. Oh, how easy it was 'in those days' to find domestic servants, and French to boot!

Jérôme came to see us almost every day. A peerless friend, so attached to us (yes, even to me) and so endearing. The Nikolai adventure gave him the opportunity to warn Gulnar: 'My dear, do not take lovers unwisely. Weigh the pros and cons first. If it is for pleasure, choose those who are well balanced and good company. If it is for utility, think carefully: Otto has many advantages which you will not find elsewhere. Don't waste your time on dull lovers. You will make better use of it by continuing your cultural education. Culture is capital that no one and no age can take away from you, and it will give you lasting pleasures, which is rarely the case with love. Don't lose your way in dreams of a great love with a great young man in possession of a great fortune. Anything can happen, even a miracle, but life is rarely perfect, doubtless to rob us of our taste for utopias. But note that it does not succeed in robbing us of our taste for the marvellous, so deeply rooted in us is our need for happiness.'

'Don't waste your time on dull lovers.' He lets me waste mine, though, with his third cousin once removed whom he considers to be at my level, I thought not without bitterness, but said nothing. He did not apply the same standards to Gulnar and to me.

'The taste for the marvellous,' Jérôme continued, 'is a marvel in itself, but it is also our poison. It allows us to bear the greyness of life and at the same time it makes us aware of this greyness through its contrast with our imagination.'

'It's a little too subtle for me, despite all your training,' Gulnar said.

'It will come.' One of Jérôme's attractive but sometimes irritating traits was his inclination towards optimism. 'It will come. But it depends more than anything on your cultivating yourselves, irrigating the particular field that is our brain. Some scholars claim we only know how to use a tenth of its capacity at most.'

He could be pedantic at times, our Jérôme.

Otto's letters were as tender as ever, but less frequent, so much so that the carefree Gulnar felt some concern—not a great deal, but enough to see how useful it would be to secure the rear with a new, wisely chosen victim. Lumbering herself with a lover to satisfy the vulgar pleasures of the flesh did not appeal to her at all—at least not for now. Flesh, the enemy of reason, would have to be reasonable, that's all. Gulnar knew how to stand firm against the adversary without sullying her charms in sordid affairs that were going nowhere.

Like a spider in her web, she waited barely a month, taking the opportunity to cultivate herself, until...

An Interesting Encounter

What a sky the Creator of Heaven and Earth stretched out that day above the racecourse: a clear, sharp sky without a single cloud and in the centre an enormous, triumphant sun which seemed to be celebrating its own advent and that of the fine weather—a festival sky. Beneath that sky the festival was indeed in full swing. Even the horses recognized it and smiled with all their teeth, quivering with joy. Yes, this was the word for the occasion: joy. For once, the pursuit of happiness had paused and happiness was there, in the grass trampled by men's big feet and ladies' pointed heels, in the top hats gleaming like advertisements for shoe polish. In the surrounding trees the birds were frolicking madly, jumping, flying, sharing the news, squabbling and joining in the general air of joyfulness.

I took part in this universal gambolling, felt light, destined for happiness, giddy like the birds under the effects of the pure, sun-soaked air.

For once, and despite the presence of Gulnar, I felt young, pretty, elegant in the strange fashion of the day: an outfit with a low waist and short skirt, topped off with a flower pot pushed down to my eyes.

'Woman,' said Alexandre Dumas *fils*, 'is a delicious creature whose life is spent disguised as a bell or sometimes a steam-roller.' At the time of this account, we were disguised as tubes, compressed and oppressed from head to toe. Our pride was not diminished by our hideous shape, nor was men's desire. Mincing, in the mistaken belief that I was the centre of the world, I waited for the photographer who was to take my pictures for a fashion magazine, which flattered my vanity excessively: for once I and not Gulnar would be the star.

Our inseparable Jérôme accompanied us, very handsome in his striped trousers and fitted jacket. Greeting an acquaintance at every step, he would tell us about the private lives of one Parisian after another, even if he didn't know them personally. The number of homosexuals strolling through the paddock seemed remarkably high, and Gulnar did not fail to draw unhappy conclusions for her own future.

'So many rivals to defeat. We're finished if we have to compete with men as well.' Then she launched into a comparative study of homosexuality. 'At home in the Caucasus that's what men were, as simple as that. Society, sociological conditions, as you say, dear Jérôme, forced them into it in some respects. As women were veiled and out of reach, they satisfied their instincts as best they could, i.e. between themselves. Let us say they became homo-sexual for lack of outlets. Just as some shepherds are said to be led astray by the devil, and use their animals. Our males were, therefore, bisexual, adapting to circumstance without remorse, and became heterosexual again after marriage. Yours, on the other hand, either plunge willingly into the drama and fear of hell when religion is involved, or, at the other extreme, believe they are essentially superior, comparing themselves conceitedly to their patrons, Oscar Wilde and the Baron de Charlus, and a host of others.'

My God, Gulnar spoke so well, blessed as she was not only with intelligence but also with the knack of choosing the most striking facts from a wealth of knowledge. And she was so elegant too, a Parisian elegance taken to perfection! She wore a black velvet suit, set off by a white blouse with a lace ruffle, and a small round hat in velvet felt with a bright-red feather attached amusingly on one side, pointing its blood-red flash at the sky. I might add that her suit came from my fashion house, where Gulnar sometimes ordered a suit or coat, which enhanced my standing not only with my fellow mannequins but also with the 'monkey', who knew we were related.

Everyone turned to look at her, while Jérôme, who, I'm sure, was in love with her in his own way, gazed fondly at her and told her she was 'bewitching', no less! And he was right: something in my cousin set her apart, and this struck even the least attentive and put her at the centre of the world. It was not Gulnar who moved there, it was the world that moved around her as though around a magnetic pole. You might think I exaggerate her attractions out of some kind of masochism, but not at all: the facts proved me right, and would always prove me right, alas.

And again I felt myself pushed to the back of the stage, to that secondary role in which I faded away as though at the bottom of a pit. And of course my joy fell flat like sails no longer billowing in the wind of hope. Suddenly wretched again, deprived even of the sun shining in the sky, again the Cinderella that no fairy godmother would come and clothe in splendour, I asked myself, what good was my youth, my mannequin's elegance, and especially this liberty I'd gained at last?

Why was I no more than this succession of moods, this chaos of opposing feelings? Like the Russian mountains, they plunged me into a ravine or returned me to the peaks, giving me joy or nausea in turn. It was exhausting to live like a cork bobbing on the waves of an always restless sea, never seeing, even in the distance, a calm horizon. Neither Gulnar nor Jérôme nor most of my relatives seemed to know these extremes, which all too often made my life unbearable and left me longing for non-existence. But perhaps the others hid those internal duels between two opposite poles, as I tried to do myself, though more often than not without success? After all, they didn't live in the shadow of a young woman in full bloom, whose radiance eclipsed me.

One should not think, though, that my feelings for Gulnar were only negative, steeped in jealousy, vexation, even hatred. Though I felt all that, I loved her, I was deeply grateful to her, I admired her, especially for her seemingly boundless generosity. She helped my father and stepmother, who at this time were living in the south, at the home of the extremely wealthy friend, the oil baron's wife whom I've already mentioned. She showered gifts on the Josézous, me, and Maryam, whose material circumstances were still deteriorating. She was affectionate and had a strong sense of family. Finally, her humour, her imagination, her charm in the strongest meaning of the word won my heart, which was nonetheless capable of hating her. 'Only God fathoms the loins and the heart'; I hope he has managed to see clearly into mine, where gold and mud alternate.

Gulnar and Jérôme did not notice my sudden despondency and chattered merrily, he playing Cicero, she the star.

'Here is Madame X.' He glanced towards a very beautiful woman with a lively, anxious face. 'She's audacious and exceptionally cynical. One day, a little the worse for wear, she explained to me that the only thing that could beat the thrill of an affair was to take part—excuse this crude word—in an "orgy"...' (Fifty years later, we would call such a gathering 'group sex'.) 'She claims that one meets important people there, and that at a single stroke one becomes intimate with several people at one go. "It's not that I enjoy it," she confided in me. "To be honest, I don't have the temperament, but one has to know what one wants." And she knows that very well. Her husband has received successive promotions and it's rumoured that he is well on the way to becoming an important ambassador. He's the man on her right; the other, on the left, is the Count of Montforgé, extremely rich, mad on horses—he's got one running here—wary of women and constantly increasing his fortune through clever manoeuvres on the Bourse.'

'Married?'

'Widowed. Father of a blonde, diaphanous daughter, the Ophelia type. He adores her and she adores him in return. Son of a dragon of a woman—strapped into her whalebone corset, she's famed throughout the Faubourg Saint-Germain, and elsewhere too. Implacable, haughty, devout.'

'In good health?'

'Which one?'

'The count, and his mother too, since we're on the subject.'

'They will live to a ripe old age. It's in the family. The father died in the war, which does even for those in the rudest of health. But what a funny question!'

Busy casting furtive glances at the count, Gulnar did not deign to reply. She observed that he looked like a grocer.

'It's very well received among the French nobility. With your outdated notions of tall, blonde Russian princes with elongated faces, you cannot conceive that there is a noble race hidden behind the girth of a Montforgé. I can tell you that he is descended from the Crusaders, the first Crusaders, I believe.'

We saw the descendant of the Crusaders take leave of his friends and approach Jérôme.

'Actually, dear monsieur, um, er, I wanted to speak to you about an interesting matter. But that is for later. In the meantime, would you do me the honour of introducing me to...'

Jérôme hastened to satisfy his request. With his overbearing courtesy, Montforgé seemed awkward to me, more than that, pompous, oozing ennui. Where was his lordly ease? Like Grandot, he trotted out platitudes but with a grandiloquent air, interspersed with numerous 'um, er's. He was the image of the classic, slightly ridiculous Frenchman in some American films: average height, well proportioned, a double chin verging on a triple, but with quite a handsome face that revealed large, dazzling white teeth when he smiled. He sported a very black moustache, which maybe he waxed like Maupassant's old dandies? His hair was greying attractively at the temples.

He did not leave our side. He followed the races, acting interested but casting sidelong glances at Gulnar when he judged the moment favourable. He was visibly impressed, though even more visibly on his guard. He must have scented the adventuress. You may find it hard to believe, but he seemed to have forgotten the horses, even his own, which was running in the race. Gulnar sensed her prey and adapted instantly to the situation. Rejecting

Mademoiselle de la Mole, she became the Princess of Cleves in person: distinguished, poetic, reserved—that's how she wanted to appear to the count, and perhaps she succeeded. As soon as she heard that the man sent by Providence was rich, titled and, oh joy, widowed, she decided he should marry her! A strategic genius responds immediately to the unexpected: in seconds, Gulnar chose the right strategy and was not to modify it until… But as a mindful and well-organized storyteller I must not get ahead of events.

The race was under way. I can think of nothing more boring than the races, which I had longed to attend, as I considered them an authentic aspect of Parisian life. The horses were running: they flew like the wind, spurred on by their jockeys; so people said, but no one could see them, as everything happened so far away, out of sight. Not that I was at all interested—it would make no difference to my life whether Amenophis II or Tutankhamun came in first. I was disconcerted, though, by the passionate reaction of the crowd: they were agitated; people ran around almost as fast as the horses, ladies screamed but kept a watchful eye on their coiffure, the loudspeakers cried at the tops of their voices… I was bored to death. What else was there for me to do here, since I had already posed for the photographer, and a fashion magazine would print the picture with the inevitable caption, 'At Longchamp Races yesterday, all eyes were on this delightful model from the House of X'? I could have left, but another role held me back: that of companion, destined to be eternally upstaged.

Attentive to the comments of the count, interspersed with 'um, er', Gulnar tilted her feather-topped head to one side in a most delicate way. It goes without saying that he asked her the traditional question, more fatal than death: 'Do you like France?'

'I love it!' she cried, enthusiasm taking her breath away. Having got it back, she repeated dramatically: 'I love it! I don't love it, I adore it! I adore everything about it and in every way: I love Camembert, the dome of the Val-de-Grâce, Racine...'

She was quoting Jérôme word for word! She gave a little laugh to show her own appreciation of her spontaneous witticism. Tenderness softened Montforgé's strong features: 'Ah, foreigners,' he said, 'no, rather, um, er, some of the most refined foreign ladies appreciate France better than some Frenchmen.'

'But of course.' Gulnar fluttered her long eyelashes modestly, and so prettily! 'I was raised by a French governess, who taught me all about your country almost before I could walk.'

Governess, my foot! I was choking with rage. Raised by the slaps of her father and the initiations of her brothers, yes; not by a French governess! When all's said and done, she had been so badly raised that I, offspring of the 'aristocratic' branch of the family, was not allowed to associate with that degenerate trio of Gulnar and her two brothers.

'What an actress!' I murmured to Jérôme, who was standing next to me using field glasses to follow the horses' progress, invisible to the naked eye. 'If the count only knew what a cynic he's courting at this moment.'

Jérôme did not share my opinion.

'Gulnar's right,' he murmured in response without looking away from the field glasses. 'Her distinction may help her with Montforgé. You wouldn't like her to start telling him her adventures, after all. I think Amenophis II is going to win.'

'I couldn't care less,' I said rudely, tears welling. I could foresee how the afternoon would end. I knew that Montforgé would sooner turn down dinner with the president of the Republic than abandon Gulnar after the races. Montforgé would not leave us, he would invite us out, devour Gulnar with his eyes as he was already doing, and would remember me only to recall I was *her* cousin. Where would he take us? 'A man in love is worse than a rabid dog,' as a proverb from my country says. Montforgé was 'bewitched', and Jérôme's comment at the start of the races had been prescient.

Once the races were over, the count launched into an interminable speech, a trying hotchpotch of words and 'um, er's, at the end of which we finally grasped his request: he was begging us to do him the great honour of accepting an impromptu dinner at his small property in Ville-d'Avray.

Gulnar allowed the begging to go on for some time. Now she was a royal, the tilt of her head, the tone of her voice showed Montforgé, should he have had any doubts, that my cousin was not a woman to leap at a free dinner or similar opportunity. Finally, judging that she had resisted for a suitable length of time, she gave in to his entreaties. Following fresh supplication, she even agreed to leave with him in his car driven by a chauffeur clad in brilliant white. As for me, Jérôme sat me in his little cabriolet where I could sulk in comfort; when he tried to make conversation, I grunted in response. 'You're hellishly difficult,' he sighed. 'It's true that one doesn't choose one's temperament.' Whereupon he gave up.

I won't recount the long evening we spent in Montforgé's little chateau, which reposed in a fairy-tale park. It wasn't really a chateau but what used to be called a folly. According to Larousse, this is the word for a pleasure pavilion 'built in town or the country at extravagant cost to satisfy a whim or to hold lovers' trysts'. It dated to the eighteenth century and had been built by a Montforgé ancestor who was given to romantic affairs. So Jérôme told us later, giving Gulnar much food for thought.

But I won't recount the evening we spent there. It was what it was bound to be: a celebration for Gulnar, a diversion for Jérôme, hell for me. But I must record what happened when we left the count after he had begged in vain to be allowed to accompany us. The car had scarcely passed through the gate of the park when Gulnar reclined nonchalantly in her seat, closed her eyes and said in a resonant voice: 'Listen to me, both of you. I am going to become the Countess of Montforgé.'

Jérôme jerked the steering wheel in shock, making the car swerve to the left. A huge vehicle just missed us and an invisible man showered us with all too audible insults, then peace was restored. Jérôme pulled over to the verge, turned towards Gulnar and gave the following speech: 'Usually, I would tell you that you're crazy. But I will tell you only this: Montforgé will never, ever marry a foreigner with neither hearth nor home, like you. To his own prejudices and immense pride, you must add the prejudices and immense pride of his mother, who would destroy her son rather than give him up to a gold digger, which, let us be honest, is what you are. Montforgé—marry a foreigner, and such a foreigner at that? Montforgé—marry a Muslim? A divorcée, who is living as the wife of a man who is himself suspect, since he maintains ties with those Bolshevik devils? A woman—'

'Whose father eats live flies by sticking them with his finger into ice cream and whose brothers are in turn, depending on the demands of the day, homosexuals, liars, thieves—'

'No, really?' Jérôme interrupted her, his voice animated with a lively and approving interest. 'You've managed to hide these picturesque details about your honourable family. Does your good father really eat live flies? For their taste or for therapeutic purposes?'

'For their taste. And he adores belching in public to entertain people. And he succeeds. I know nothing more amusing than my father's belching.'

'What a shame he has stayed in the Caucasus. I am sure that the Count of Montforgé would have appreciated these exotic methods of diverting society. Amusements in France are so dull.'

'You are quite right,' Gulnar sighed. 'So to brighten the count's last years, I'm going to marry him.'

'Dear, inestimable Gulnar, whom I love and appreciate more than you imagine, you should understand that you have as much chance of marrying Montforgé as I do of changing into a donkey before your eyes.'

'Rest assured, it is done: you are a donkey. The Count of Montforgé will marry me despite my brothers, my father, my loose behaviour, my religion, etc. etc. Would you like to bet on it, the stake remaining at the discretion of the winner?'

'Any stake is fine for me. And you may rest assured that I will not abuse the opportunity.'

'Very well, let's say that you will have won if after one year I have not made Montforgé marry me.'

'Done. But my poor Gulnar, brilliant pupil, with a remarkable wit but too optimistic, because you are an exceptional woman you think you possess the world, which does not let itself be taken so easily. Another detail: it is the monster of the Faubourg Saint-Germain who holds the greater part of the fortune, a considerable fortune inherited from her American mother. She buried her mother and kept the fortune. If necessary, the battleaxe could disinherit a son led astray, who may be rich in his own right but is poor, if I may say so, compared to her. Moreover, I should remind you that Montforgé is some thirty years older than you.'

'Oh, I'm used to it. It won't bother me. Quite the reverse, he will die more quickly, leaving me a widow in the prime of life.'

'A false hope. I've already told you that members of this noble family live to a ripe old age, to the great displeasure of their heirs.'

'Too bad! At a pinch I could demand a divorce, if I think he's obstinately clinging on to life. He would have to grant me a few small millions.'

Having run out of arguments, Jérôme restarted the car, which purred down the dark road. Gulnar was silent, Jérôme too, while I dreamt the kind of dreams that always betray us: beautiful celebrations that in life turn into crude sideshows; love affairs that dissolve in vinegar; the difficult task of living of which Fontenelle spoke so well. The bitterness that underpinned my soul gave itself free rein.

We crossed a bridge and drove into the Bois de Boulogne. As we entered the forest, Gulnar woke up and declared her desire to go and see José and Zuleykha.

'It's almost midnight,' Jérôme observed.

'What does it matter? They always go to bed late on Sundays and love to have visitors. They'll be delighted to see us.'

'Ever the optimist,' said Jérôme. 'But I'm happy to take you there.'

Recently, we had visited the Josézous less often—José had not been very welcoming. Not to beat about the bush, he criticized us for our 'whoring', as he put it so prettily, a criticism he directed in particular at Gulnar. Almeria didn't come to see him so often, as he was afraid of bumping into her; yes, yes, José knew she hadn't slept with Almeria, but she had treated him very badly. He also knew the story about Karpov and was outraged. Who would be the next victim? He had previously attacked Gulnar several times in a fit of rage: 'If you want to play the femme fatale, go ahead, but hunt your prey somewhere else, not here. I'm sick of these courtesans roaring past in their motor cars as they try to impress us. Your poor husband too! What are you doing to him? Aren't you ashamed?'

As we drew nearer to my spirited brother-in-law's home, I had a flash of intuition: Gulnar wanted to tell the Josézous that she had found better elsewhere. She would tell them about her designs on Montforgé.

She'd been right, as we found a large gathering in the studio with pale, dishevelled Almeria in the middle. Smelling of alcohol and defeat, he glided across the ring cape in hand, but stopped dead when he saw us and disappeared into a dark corner from which he didn't emerge. Magnificent and outrageous, Shamsi presided over the assembly with his customary arrogance. He proudly showed us the holes in his trousers which Maryam had not had time to patch; their location was such that essential parts of his person threatened to escape at the slightest injudicious movement. These holes were the star attraction of the evening: he showed them off smugly, constantly drawing everyone's attention to them, taking a strange pleasure in flaunting his destitution, as though, wanting to be great in all things, even his poverty had to be epic. He succeeded to a certain extent. Chased from one apartment to another for non-payment of rent—the apartment becoming smaller and uglier with every move—besieged by bailiffs, creditors, tax demands, he and my sister had ended up in a dubious hotel which Shamsi boastfully called his 'current residence'. Whole streets in the sixteenth arrondissement were off limits, as outstanding debts lay in wait for them like monsters lurking behind the cash registers. How did they survive? By selling all that they had left to sell, which was shrinking to nothing.

Following the classic process, objects had been sold off in decreasing order of value, beginning with jewels, moving on to mere valuables, and ending in the disposal of furs and clothes. Shamsi had sold his last overcoat, for which he'd paid an exorbitant price in London, and since then had walked defiantly, even when very cold, with his raincoat slung casually over his arm to show that he had no need of a coat, not even of one so light. Poor Maryam—the main victim in this lamentable debacle—soldiered on without complaint, but there was just one stroke of good fortune: the English nanny engaged for their newborn son just after they had emigrated was so devoted to him that she offered to take responsibility for him. Maryam was in no position to refuse, so the nanny took the child to the south of France, where she settled down with a husband found in Paris, saving this offspring of the emigration from an uncertain fate. Childless herself, the nanny raised the boy as her own and Maryam became a sort of titular mother, attached to her son by the umbilical cord of the post office. Emigration created thousands of sad cases of this kind.

Please excuse this digression, as we return to the studio.

Gulnar was waiting for only one thing: for the departure of the strangers gathered around the Josézous, so that she could share her heartfelt hopes. She settled in a corner of the couch, her whole attitude conveying her desire to see the intruders decamp. She did such a good job that half an hour later only family were left, apart from one outsider, Jérôme, who was to drive us home.

Then Gulnar sat up and said nonchalantly, 'I want you to know that I have just made a conquest that I hope will take me far: that of the Count of Montforgé, whom Jérôme introduced to me at the races. You know how extremely rich he is: racing stables, finance, chateaux, etc.' She gave Shamsi a taunting look, as she knew his fondness for social status and titles.

He shrugged disdainfully. 'The Count of Montforgé? Never heard of him. I would like to examine his degree of nobility. At home in St Petersburg—'

'We couldn't care less about St Petersburg,' Gulnar interrupted brutally. 'Petersburg is dead and so are its princes and counts and all your former glory. And you'd do better to take any job, instead of harping on about all these corpses and showing off the holes in your trousers.'

The atmosphere was ruined. Shamsi turned white as a sheet. 'Poor idiot!' He struggled to maintain his dignity. 'Poor imbecile! She's hardly out of the barbarous backwoods of Baku and she thinks she's emancipated! She plays the fine lady and picks up fake counts at the races.'

'I haven't picked up anyone. It was the Count of Montforgé who noticed me and asked Jérôme to make the introductions. It also happens that you're a bey, which I might add is a ridiculous title and doesn't stop you flaring your enormous nostrils.'

It's true that he did have enormous nostrils, eyes elongated like a Mongolian's and teeth that would have graced a horse, all belonging to the Tartars of the steppes who razed cities to the ground and killed every living creature except their horses. It's true that he looked far more barbaric than Gulnar.

'Dear Jérôme,' said Shamsi, turning to our friend, 'I'm afraid to say that your determination to serve as guide to these useless girls does you no honours.'

'That is true,' José opined. 'My poor Jérôme, you're wasting your time.'

José always shared Shamsi's opinions. In this instance he did so wholeheartedly, since, as I've said, he disapproved of our behaviour and feared it would have a bad influence on his wife. Meanwhile, Zuleykha was listening intently.

'And the Count of Mon-thingumajig has fallen in love with you?' she asked, her curiosity piqued. 'Just like that, in a flash?'

'A whirlwind, yes. And he wants me to marry him—no, I want him to marry me,' she corrected herself, not risking too many lies before these witnesses.

Shamsi and José burst out laughing simultaneously, as offensively as possible.

'You wouldn't like to make a play for the president of the United States while you're at it, would you?' José asked. 'He doesn't have a title like your count, but does have a very comfortable position and first-class political power. You should give it some serious thought.'

She had always got on his nerves. I had thought for a while that he was starting to hate her. He hated what he saw as her disreputable behaviour. He hated her frivolity, her desire to show off and what he called her new literary mania. She had bent his ear about Mademoiselle Aïssé, claimed she could already feel the stirring of a book in her breast—which was clearly the height of pretension—and always put herself at the forefront, etc. There wasn't a grievance he hadn't thrown in her face, often unfairly.

'You can laugh all you like,' Gulnar said, in no way disconcerted. 'You'll still admire me one day.'

The siege began on the morrow of this memorable day, but who was laying siege to whom? Montforgé must have naively thought he was the besieger, not suspecting that he was the one under siege. So, the day after this meeting, he began what he imagined was his siege by sending a basket of red roses the size of a newborn's cradle. Seemingly moved, Gulnar smelt the flowers and read in them a message giving notice of her victory. 'Say it with flowers.' The florists were right.

That very day she began to prepare for the social ascent that she knew awaited her: she chose a less striking hairstyle, wore her make-up more discreetly, and adopted a modest bearing in anticipation of her meeting with the battleaxe of the Faubourg Saint-Germain. She was able to fly to victory on the wings of imagination, without pessimism to hold her back. It was a great strength, which doubtless increased her charm, though she was unaware of it. She was so much the opposite of languid, anxious and uncertain that the gaiety she emanated attracted and enchanted people. Yes, I think this explanation holds one of the keys to her success.

So sure was she of victory that she began to work feverishly on her English, which she didn't know well and which she considered indispensable to her future social status as a countess. She adopted a permanently gentle, distant air towards the count, wrapping herself in a protective cloak of virtue. Yes, her main weapon in the subjugation of Montforgé was her supposed virtue.

They saw one another every day for a month. Montforgé either came to us or he went out with Gulnar, first with Jérôme and me, then just the two of them. But he did not invite her to his hotel in the Rue Saint-Dominique where he lived with his mother. Gulnar was furious about this, though it was basic self-preservation.

'Of course, one does not introduce someone like me to one's family. All well and good. But Henri, Count of Montforgé can dissolve in tears at my feet and he will not have me. We will see who will have whom.'

'My dear Gulnar, "who will have whom" is not very French and is ugly on the ear. Mademoiselle Aïssé-in-waiting should avoid such unfortunate turns of phrase.'

'Very well, very well,' Gulnar replied, irritated. For the moment she was more preoccupied with the future Gulnar of Montforgé than Gulnar alias Aïssé.

'I warned you of the obstacles you would face. Let me tell you that yesterday at the Jockey Club Montforgé asked me many questions about Otto, you, your past. When he asked whether your relations with Otto were conjugal or extra-marital, I said nothing precise, for the obvious reason that I know nothing precise. But to salve your potential wounds, I can tell you I have never seen a man so madly in love. When he talks about you, he is transfigured, literally, and the oaf that you know changes into a mystic sensing union with God.'

'Don't make fun of me,' Gulnar said, having lost none of her sense of irony.

'I'm teasing you a little, but our dear Montforgé really is losing his head a little.'

'He needs to lose it altogether or I will slip from his grasp.'

Throughout this month of siege (I'll repeat the question: of whom by whom?) he sent flowers every other day. Each arrival was larger, more beautiful, more fragrant than the last. The clutter of baskets and outsized bouquets gave our apartment the air of a florist's shop, literally so, as we were enveloped in a heavy scent that gave us migraines. While in the beginning Gulnar was delighted at these signs of attention, she ended up disgusted with them: weren't they some kind of proof of her powerlessness to obtain better? Gentle and distant, she ended up begging Montforgé to stop this deluge.

'I no longer know where to put these wonders. And by filling our home with their scent they'll end up turning my head.'

'Oh, if only that were true,' Montforgé quipped, which was a rarity for him. 'But, um, er, if you permit me, I will bring you something else tomorrow.'

Gulnar wracked her brains to guess what this 'something else' could be. Was it an invitation from his mother?

The next day he came to pick up Gulnar to take her to the theatre. Jérôme had spent the afternoon with her and was still there when the count took a small box out of his pocket, as though it was an entirely natural gesture requiring no introduction or explanation, and handed it to Gulnar.

'Since, um, er, you are tired of real flowers, I have taken the liberty of bringing you one which will not bother you with its scent.'

He sat down heavily, waiting for Gulnar's ecstatic reaction. He was such a bad psychologist!

Gulnar opened the box and we saw a brooch of diamonds in the shape of a rose, a large ruby shining in the middle of its petals. This princely jewel came from Cartier. Gulnar closed the box with a snap and put it on the table next to Montforgé.

'Monsieur,' she said—it was no longer the Princess of Cleves speaking, but Marie Antoinette, the queen of France, who astounded the Duke of Rohan with her disdain—'Monsieur,' Gulnar repeated, lifting her head proudly—Montforgé shifted uncomfortably in his chair—'Until now, I did not know what you thought of me, and that you held me in such low esteem. Your gesture is so eloquent that it requires no commentary: you take me for a woman who can be bought with jewels.'

The count let out a dramatic 'Oh!', but Gulnar took no notice.

'Monsieur, let me tell you that I am loved by a man and I love him in return as he deserves, that is to say, very much. He will take it badly if I relented and accepted gifts of this value from anyone other than him. I am hurt that you are so mistaken about me. I did not think you are capable of it.' (Jérôme winced in pain at the poor sequence of tenses, especially unfortunate in a speech of such solemnity.)

She rose, and a very pale Montforgé did the same.

'You will understand that I prefer not to go out with you this evening.'

And Marie Antoinette, the offended queen of France, acknowledged the Duke of Rohan with a scarcely perceptible nod of the head and left us.

I had never seen a man in such a piteous state. Montforgé seemed to stagger on his rather short legs. Pale at first, he regained colour: his rather short, pinkish neck turned red, and beads of sweat covered the large, clear-cut features of his face.

'I don't understand, um, er, I really don't understand. Why has Gulnar taken a friendly gesture so badly? I thought she liked me. Yes, I forgot the husband… I forgot the reactions of an overly sensitive woman. Jérôme… What do you think?' He needed to feel supported, his mind put at rest by our sympathy. He sought to draw closer to us, as we were close to Gulnar.

'I've been stupid,' he said, continuing his defence, falling back limply in his chair. He was having difficulty breathing and I wondered, alarmed, if he would have the poor taste to suffer an apoplectic fit in front of us. What were we to do? Would he give way to tears? For a descendant of the Crusaders, he lacked composure.

An image flashed through my mind: I saw one of his Crusader ancestors defeated by Saladin at Jerusalem, disarmed, thrown to the ground, begging for mercy, just as his descendant was begging for mercy here in Paris from a Muslim who may have descended by some convoluted route from a grand Arab conqueror. Anything was possible in the complicated game of history, which wove and unravelled the threads of fate, the destinies of millions—and in the more complicated history of our genes.

'Jérôme,' cried the count almost madly, 'go and tell Gulnar of my despair. Beg her to forgive me. Please convey to her my apologies and my veneration.'

His veneration! God, I thought, how love makes idiots of men by scrambling their brains. What a masterful performance from Gulnar. She had surpassed herself, discovering for herself and revealing to us her talents as an actress.

'It's perhaps not the right moment,' Jérôme replied with gravitas, joining in his protégée's game. 'I will do it, but later, when she has calmed down.'

'So what should I do? Stay or go?'

'I think it would be wiser to go.'

Montforgé slipped the fatal box into his pocket with disgust, as though it were a sick animal. He proffered a dozen 'um, er's, then, miserable and dejected, left us. Hardly had the door closed behind him than Gulnar appeared, radiant.

'I hope you appreciated my subtle game! Ah yes, Henri, Count of Montforgé imagines I would become his mistress at little cost, when I want his name and nothing else. Was he very affected?'

'Affected in the very depths of his soul. Shaken to his core, having swallowed his bitter drink to the last drop.'

Jérôme laughed, Gulnar laughed, I laughed. Montforgé's guardian angel himself must have laughed at the recollection of his miserable air and the gap between his sorrow and its cause.

'Now that we've had our fun,' Jérôme said, 'allow me to tell you, incomparable Gulnar, that the divine Sarah herself would have applauded just now. Though I find your game, or what you call your game, quite… I am looking for an epithet that is not too severe… let us say questionable. Though you are close to a charming man, goodness personified, you are behaving like a, shall we say, harlot.' (Fifty years ago one could still use such an old-fashioned word.)

'Aren't I one?' Gulnar replied candidly. 'Don't talk to me about Otto's affection and the suffering I would inflict on him if my policy with Montforgé proves "successful".' (This word Gulnar said in English, as she liked to pepper her speeches with the language now that she was studying it.) 'I cannot spend my whole life with Otto after all, and probably not with Montforgé either, and especially not if I marry him. I don't like him all that much, to be honest. And I don't think I'm good at marriage, at living as a couple and sharing everything come what may: bed, meals, bank account, until death us do part. The boredom, the routine, the deadly dullness that marriage engenders—I've seen it so often. It defeats the best resolutions, the most beautiful love affairs.'

Jérôme gave a smile of pleasure. He must have approved of the structure of this monologue, and perhaps its content too.

'In short,'—this was Jérôme speaking—'you agree with Napoleon that "marriage is an exchange of bad temper during the day and bad odours during the night".'

I would like to tell you a little more about Gulnar's charm: I put so badly into words what I sense through intuition. The marrow of life, like that of man, is locked away behind defences that are hard to penetrate; you scratch, you dig, but you do not reach what is essential. This is how I have never been able to penetrate to the essence of Gulnar, who more than the average person is a striking tangle of virtues and faults. Seeing her ardour for life, her determination to gather the flowers of life, I am always reminded of the words of Nietzsche that I read at that time: 'Life for us means to transform constantly into light and flame all that we are and all that we meet with.'

I am aware of the incongruity of applying such great words to a pretty arriviste, one woman among millions looking for success. But she knew exactly how to avoid banality through her inner fire, which transfigured her most trivial words and deeds, lending them an attraction that was hard to define. Yes, I know I'm repeating myself. Maybe I'm doing it more for myself than the reader, in order to understand how one can live so basely yet appear to soar so high.

'And what I also find appalling, to be frank,' Jérôme resumed, 'is that you dream of marriage while also dreaming that it will be of brief duration. Is it desirable to torture two men, Otto and Montforgé, for such fleeting success?'

'The marriage would be fleeting, not the success: I would have married a Parisian personality, a very rich man. He will give me an honourable nationality and a considerable fortune. And who says that I will divorce as soon as I'm married? The count may have the tact to depart this life without waiting for my old age. Don't you find that he is often a high colour?'

'You're abominable. Siren of Baku, what would you have been if you had remained veiled, hidden away in the harem? It is true that I would have been the first to regret it. And what tactic have you devised in your calculating brain?'

'To refuse to see him until he is bitterly convinced of my virtue; until he sweats regret from all his pores, until despair makes him confront his monster of a mother.'

*

The day after his faux pas Montforgé begged Jérôme to intercede with Marie Antoinette, who was refusing to listen to his pleading and remained as unbending as a bronze statue. She also refused to reply to a four-page letter, written in a tiny hand in which the count praised her to the skies and abased himself to the level of the gutter. He had to cut short his efforts, because of an unexpected event for all the actors in the play: Otto returned, but not without warning, as he was too polite and too prudent to run the risk of a sudden intrusion with unforeseen consequences. He sent us a telegram twenty-four hours before his departure. This resumption of conjugal (or nearly conjugal) relations suited Gulnar wonderfully: she became a married woman again, respectable, fully immersed in virtue and duty, very happy to live out a tranquil love story with her husband who respected her while a nasty man who hoped to bring about her fall—in the moral sense, that is—was moping somewhere in his hotel on the Rue Saint-Dominique in the company of his domineering mother. Informed about the situation by Jérôme, the man of vice kept quiet during the long month that Otto spent with us.

Otto had returned to us thinner, melancholic, already carrying within himself the sorrow that lay in wait for him. More than ever, he inspired my compassion, as I sensed that he felt true affection for Gulnar beyond their passionate affair. He 'wished her well', in the pure sense of the term, wishing her happiness, even if it was with someone other than him.

His saintly disposition did not remain in words only. During this trip, which was to be his last, Otto deposited a very large sum in Gulnar's name, as he was worried about her future. He felt himself old and at the mercy of age and an uncertain fate, and had difficulty concealing his anxiety. Otto was a striking example to me of the reality of premonitions.

And what became of me, while Gulnar juggled with the destiny of two men? Oh, nothing much. I continued my liaison with Grandot, so deeply unsatisfactory—today we would say 'frustrating'—and my work at the Place Vendôme. Fortunately, now that I had a lover like every one of these ladies, I was considered less of a simpleton.

'Showing some sense at last!' exclaimed Mary, on hearing the good news. She was, though, going through a phase of intense disgust, with men whom she replaced—to her advantage, she said—with all sorts of substitutes which I cannot detail in these pages, in protest against the hurricane of pornography sweeping over our permissive society. Suffice it for the reader to know that Mary's imagination defied that of the most inventive novelists and one could only regret her failure to put it to better use.

She was also an accomplished storyteller, lingering over wildly obscene details. I suspected her of dwelling on them solely in order to shock the 'lady', who would react violently.

'Enough!' she would cry. 'I don't want to hear such filth. If you carry on, I'll complain to the *patron*.'

'Ooh, what a ninny! Go and tell tales if you want. She's had lovers in spades, and acts so high and mighty!'

'I've only had eighteen lovers,' the 'lady' said with dignity.

Fond of order in everything, she kept exact accounts even on this subject, in which it's excusable to lose one's head. She never lost hers, which was stuffed with conventions and small, sensible calculations.

'Tell me, then,' said Mary, 'what do you want us to talk about? Broderie anglaise and growing roses? All very nice but not very profitable. At least we sometimes get some pleasure and a few pennies from these wretched men. Come on, Mouse, tell us about your great romance with your medicine man.'

To distance myself from the 'lady' and her hypocritical prudery, I went into detail about Grandot in a more relaxed fashion, taking advantage of Jérôme's absence. I complained of the monotony of our relationship, and how I tried to interrupt it with my fierce sarcasm, my meanness and arguments that I could skilfully start and maintain to dispel my boredom.

'We have to behave gently with men. That's women's role,' the 'lady' declared sententiously.

Mary sneered unceremoniously. Lucie imitated her out of respect. I maintained the general tone and the dresser followed the crowd. The 'lady' shrugged her shoulders, pursed her lips and kept a bitter silence.

No, I will not record other samples of our conversations, which were pretty monotonous too, except when Mary introduced some flight of fancy, which might take the form of an electric dryer or other aphrodisiac aid.

Once I was used to the journey, I went to Orléans on my own. I would take the train on Saturday afternoon and would be met at Orléans-les-Aubrais station by Grandot, if he was not busy hacking innocent flesh, or Clément, a true jack of all trades: valet, chauffeur, gardener, beater for the hunt and I don't know what else.

We would set off at a gallop in the ten-horsepower motor car towards Orléans. We would arrive in the deserted street, and already from afar a look of unspeakable ennui would spread across my face. The smell of polished wood in the entrance hall, the incense paper in the bedroom, which Grandot, still in love with orientalism, never forgot to burn before my arrival, that air of eternal peace that one finds in village cemeteries would envelop me, hold me in its grip, mummify me, for a while at least. I had to resist falling asleep in the charm of passivity, the neighbour of stupidity. Yes, charm... I caught myself sometimes, dreaming of living out my days in this warm quietness, at Grandot's side, without excitement but also without troubles. To sleep a great deal, to abandon absurd hopes and vain actions; to lead an existence without lustre, with only death to look forward to at the end of the road. To live with one's eyes closed, ears stopped up, mind bound; to live one's life on hold. Lassitude, the fear of life, seemed to have me in its grip already. And what could I hope for? Next to Gulnar's attractive sun I was an extinguished star. Why not age gently, in this smell of wood that I adored, in the shadow of this ancient cathedral that would mark the hours of my life by the call of its bells and the chime of its clocks? I note in passing that I never went into this honourable edifice where the faithful addressed their prayers to a Christian God and his prophet Jesus. For it never occurred to me that he might be anything other than a prophet.

I have never spoken of Gulnar's attitude towards religion, or mine. I think my cousin was not disposed towards what might be defined broadly and in sum as a sense of God or a sense of wonder. The splendours of the earth, the succession of new, intense pleasures, the admiration of men, absorbed her completely without leaving any room for aspirations that were not concrete, diverting her from vague dreams, which for stormy temperaments like hers are a waste of time.

And me? What did I see in myself? A hazy religiosity that, when I try to analyse it retrospectively, looks like a collection of superstitions, made concrete in a minuscule Koran, a real amulet that never left me. It was a magic talisman that was supposed to obtain for me, without any involvement on my part—I mean to say, without any moral or spiritual effort on my part—whatever I asked of it. How could I reach Allah, this Transcendence to which nothing bound me? And the Prophet Mohammed? Nothing bound me either to this Arab-born prophet who had shut away my peers behind a veil. Some said we had misinterpreted his words: perhaps so, but the fact remained, and I thanked that unknown Allah for delivering me from a piece of cloth that cuts you off from the world, casting you into a prison.

Often, when Grandot was out attending to a patient, I remained alone in the room lit by the pink lampshade, tinged with blue by my friend's romantic fumigations. I would lie on the pink bed and let time pass, without smell or noise or substance but more indestructible than the most resistant material. Sometimes I would go back to the past, but would hastily chase away its resurgence, thanking the Heavens for delivering me. More often, I would go into the future, locked in its mystery; sometimes too, empty of thoughts and even of dreams, free, I would dwell in the present and become bored, listening to the hours chime from the top of the cathedral, the only sound in the suffocating silence of the house. And what a few moments ago had appeared desirable—my life and death in this place—suddenly seemed so horrible in its mortal stagnation that anxiety gripped me by the throat and I was filled with the desire to flee. What, end my life here, perhaps a long life, in the torpor of semi-death? What, to have escaped the confinement of my Muslim sisters by the chance offered by a world war and unprecedented revolution, only to submit to another, almost the same? No, my whole being refused, and too bad for the lost quietness, for the risks, the problems, the disappointments of freedom; I would not refuse to pay the highest price for freedom, that so often poisoned gift.

Grandot would return and we would resume our limping relationship, dominated by all kinds of incompatibility, which led to constant clashes. Whatever he said, he seemed stupid to me, even when by chance he showed himself to be intelligent, so incurable was my contempt for this man who was not in the least contemptible, but who lacked taste, culture, wit. When he didn't speak, he annoyed me; when he did speak, I was sarcastic. To escape this disharmony from which we both suffered, but in different ways, we would resort to physical love, though with the best will in the world it was soon exhausted. I knew I should break off this ridiculous relationship—and he certainly knew it too—but I could not find the courage. To leave this first lover whom I had accepted after a struggle against myself required a determination that I was not capable of at that time. Moreover, even such an ambiguous love affair was still love; it still satisfied the need to love and be loved which we often attach to the first object to come along, because we have to meet this need at any cost. I remembered something Jérôme once said: 'In this respect, almost all beings are interchangeable; what does not change is our thirst for love.'

A final insight, the most damning for me, into my character made me understand why I still clung to Grandot: he gave me the opportunity to exert on a living person all the unconscious meanness that simmered within me and was intensified by contact with him. Since he cried easily and had only the most humdrum things to say, I loved to inspire his tears and feed my contempt by listening to him speak.

Why didn't Grandot send me packing? Because there were compensations, I think: my taste for physical love, which he had revealed to me, and, sometimes, my sudden tenderness, all the more intense for being rarely expressed. What's more, I was twenty years his junior, and I combined in his eyes the double prestige of a Parisian mannequin and the most authentic exoticism. Why not say too that I was pretty—at least in the eyes of others, because I didn't like my features, which were very pronounced in my youth.

During the weekends in Orléans, I would go hunting with Grandot in the Sologne that overwhelmed all my senses: hearing, sight, smell. I loved the solitude of the forest, the humid sky, the birdsong, the scent of the earth. How different it all was from the scorched countryside of my childhood, the bright, contrasting colours, with the Caspian as the backdrop. I was to find its indigo blue later, in the south of France. It was all mist in the Sologne, still waters in the ponds, a delicate shade of grey. My favourite spot was a tiny pond ringed with reeds that parted on one bank to make room for a toy boat. I would hop into it and settle down to watch the clouds chase one another across the watery sky. Meanwhile, Grandot and his friends were hunting. I would hear gunshots moving closer or further away and think about the animals destined to die.

One day, Grandot gave me a pretty little rifle in the hope that I would gain a taste for hunting. First I had to learn to aim, and to that end he tied an unfortunate hare to a tree and taught me the art of killing. The hare writhed in panic, sensing its imminent demise. I shot. I missed. I started again, I missed again. At the fourth attempt I hit him in the side and, no longer able to writhe, the little animal twitched in an attempt to escape death, which arrived with a loud bang.

I fired another shot without hitting the small lump, which was slowly turning red with blood. Then I threw down the rifle and burst into tears of disgust and shame.

This fifty-year-old memory convinces me of one fact that I have tended to doubt: that we change, that the experience of life changes us without our realizing. Today, nothing in the world would compel me to shoot a tethered, defenceless creature. That young woman, that former self, remains an astonishing enigma to me; I don't understand her any better than I would a stranger. How could she aim at and shoot a small animal that was at her mercy? Out of curiosity or cruelty, or because it was the thing to do?

Today's me cannot find an explanation and remains perplexed at this incomprehensible me, the two linked nevertheless by a mysterious bond, physical more than intangible, which passes through all the storms of life intact, protecting thereby the permanence of my fate.

When it became unbearably cold in the forest, I would follow the paths to a farm where I would find a great fire burning in the old hearth and where Grandot would join me sooner or later, alone or with his friends. He would brag of his hunting success, sit by the fire and enjoy the wine and omelette provided by the farmer's wife, a fat, grubby woman who never stopped complaining about the high cost of living.

The flames made the wood crackle, smoked the ham and sausages hanging in the fireplace and cast a red glow over the muzzles of the dogs lying at our feet. Grandot wanted to embrace me, because the extreme heat after the cold relaxed him and rekindled his sentimentality, which I hated, especially in public. I became mean again and he became unhappy.

We would return by car, ghostly clumps of bare trees looming over the dark road. From time to time the red glow of a farm would pierce the black night and I would feel a rush of well-being at the thought of the warm house waiting for us, surrounded by a town and protected against the icy hostility of nature. I always thought of the millions of animals and their wretched condition, especially in winter: pursued by hunger, cold, men. A sense of security, deceptive in reality, soothed my soul, inclined me to indulge Grandot for a few hours. For a very few hours.

We would go to bed very early, because we still felt a carnal urge for each other, and because the next day I had to rise at dawn to take the train that would allow me to reach my work at nine o'clock. From the Gare d'Orsay I had only to cross the Tuileries to reach the Place Vendôme—yes, 'in those days' that's where the Orléans trains came in.

I'm going to jump from my winter love with Grandot to our summer love, to our only holiday together, a twelve-day road trip in Savoy. The attentive reader will have noticed that I juggle with seasons, months, even years. These distant memories do not follow an exact chronology in my mind; they are jumbled, if not in their content then in their sequence. What I know for certain is that my love affair lasted a whole calendar year, unfolded against the backdrop of the four seasons, each giving it its particular scent.

*

We left Orléans early on a fine June morning, and as the sacred hour (lunchtime) approached the sordid truth dawned on me: economy was to be the watchword of this trip. When we arrived in a village or town, we would wander from restaurant to inn, from inn to hotel, searching not for lost time but for the best deal. Grandot did not trust the Michelin guide and prudently wanted to see for himself the menu displayed at the doors.

I took a voluptuous pleasure in hating him whenever he was lost in laborious accounts, studying them for a long time, making calculations and reaching a tentative conclusion before determining his choice. He was wary of confidence tricks, and would never be fooled by them. Accustomed since childhood to the avarice that reigned in my oil magnate family, I should have indulged Grandot in this respect. But my family's avarice did not repel me. Why not? Is it because, considerable though it was, it was highly imaginative? Is it because the members of my family afflicted by this misfortune were very colourful characters, and a colourful character benefits from colour even when it comes to his faults? My maternal grandfather, one of the richest men in the Caucasus, donated fabulous sums to charitable works, but flinched at the thought of giving a dinner or losing a few roubles in a game, which encouraged his entourage to trick him as best they could to emerge the winner. My paternal grandmother shed tears over every kopek destined for the purchase of food, but did not hesitate to take a precious ring off her finger to offer it to a guest. My aunts, my uncles, my cousins were mean, but in an entertaining way. At least that's how it seems to me through the fog of decades, and perhaps not impartially.

Grandot, bland, mawkish and petit bourgeois, though he wasn't in terms of social standing, seemed to suffer from a second-rate avarice, sullied once again by ridiculousness. I had long suspected him of it without it bothering me, because the fault was barely noticeable in the customary run of events. In Paris we always went to the same restaurants, which ruled out choice and therefore posed no problem. In Orléans too, our set pattern of life did not pose any difficulties. His tendency to talk about prices, money and savings did irritate me, but since everything about him irritated me, I didn't consider it important.

On this first and last trip that I took with him, I saw his miserliness at work and could track the smallest signs of it at my leisure. I found his loud joy when he discovered a comfortable hotel for a modest price, which 'in those days' was not rare, oppressive. He would show me the bill, comment on it and take it away to savour it some more on the road. It inspired in him a respect for the body of hoteliers and for humanity in general, whom he began to doubt whenever he considered their prices exorbitant.

One evening in Evian, from our hotel room (modest prices, decent comfort) situated at the edge of the lake, we watched the sun set over Lake Geneva in an atmosphere of calm beauty that inclined us to peace and love. Forgetting Grandot's faults, my heart turned to him in a great surge of affection: the tenderness he felt for me despite my hostility seemed to me a great quality that I was wrong to disregard. Suddenly I felt so ashamed that I threw myself into his arms in tears: for him, for me, for the imperfection of the world, which reflected the imperfection of our feelings. 'I do not do the good I want to do.' An old lament on human relationships. Seeing me cry, Grandot cried too. I've already mentioned his propensity for tears: weak and emotional, the slightest sentimental incident, the slightest appeal to his heart would devastate him. Gripped by the pressing need to know I was loved, I asked him if he loved me and he effusively assured me he did. Then he wept again, even more than before. Later, remembering that scene, both grotesque and touching, I could see all Grandot's duplicity, and I realized that there was remorse in his tears too. Having already resolved at that time to marry a woman 'from his circle' and richly endowed, he knew he would leave me, his awkward, capricious mistress without fortune or connections.

Almost certain to be accepted by the other, he had nonetheless undertaken this farewell trip that would close an amorous interlude from which he had drawn little joy. And I've never held this apparent duplicity against him, as in his way he still loved me. I think it likely that he loved me a great deal at the start of our liaison. He had even gone as far as to speak of marriage, though admittedly with hesitation.

My recollections of that holiday are confused: the days are linked by Grandot's valiant efforts to reduce expenditure, while the evening on Lake Geneva, when my soul trembled with fleeting tenderness, surfaces like a small island in the troubled waters of my memory. I was happy when the disappointing holiday, the disappointing cohabitation with Grandot, came to an end. I knew more than ever that our bond had been a delusion, but had still felt incapable of breaking it. Is it because, thanks to my inner demons, I enjoyed the hatred that Grandot so often inspired in me? It's not impossible.

*

I was glad to return to Paris, and to Gulnar. Her cheerful presence, her calm cynicism, her generosity with money created a total change in atmosphere from Grandot. What was the state of her relationship with Montforgé? I must go back in time now, as what I'm about to narrate happened before my holiday with my unhappy lover.

We left off at the 'affair of the necklace', that is, the affair of the rose-shaped brooch, and Montforgé's discomfort at Otto's unexpected arrival, which had allowed Gulnar to resume her life of virtue at the side of a man who indeed respected her.

Otto stayed a whole month with us, and left one morning when I was working, which meant I could not accompany him to the station with Gulnar. We said our farewells at home, face to face, he and I. He clasped me in his arms for a long time and implored me, 'Dear friend, take care of Gulnar. I fear for her.'

I parted from him with a haunting sense of guilt. He feared for her… what kind of illusion was he living in? I felt at fault and absurd, aware of all the harm Gulnar hoped to cause him soon, and felt myself complicit in a crime.

Hardly had he gone than Montforgé, kept up to date by Jérôme, begged him to intercede with Gulnar to obtain her pardon. She let herself be beseeched for two whole weeks, the period of time she judged necessary to make the count stew in a soup of remorse, hope and lust. Then she relented, on condition that she receive him in my and Jérôme's presence. In a solemn scene, she wanted 'to take stock of her relations with Montforgé', an expression that she employed pompously, very pleased with her own eloquence. Gulnar's mind was increasingly free of the pangs of doubt.

Montforgé returned to us one evening with two almost modest bouquets; one for Gulnar and one for me. This gesture marked the end of the great offensives and the inauguration of an era of reason and moderation. He kissed our hands with the same air of protocol, with an identical kiss, lest he arouse the suspicion of a guilty preference. The conversation began with trivia, which we dwelt on easily, especially Jérôme, who feared stormy explanations. Thanks to his flexibility and the endless number of frivolous or serious subjects he held in reserve, this neutral conversation could have gone on for a long time. But Gulnar threw a clarification, a warning, an injunction in the direction of the count, and, taking advantage of a moment's silence, becoming Marie Antoinette once again, she looked Montforgé directly in the eye and declared in a haughty voice: 'Monsieur!'

The Duke of Rohan flinched at her tone of voice, froze beneath the queen's gaze and waited, hunched in on himself.

Yes, I am exaggerating, but though he did not actually make these particular gestures, the count's attitude eloquently suggested them.

'I am happy to have it out with you before my cousin and Jérôme: my words will have more weight in the presence of such witnesses. Oh, this won't take long... You were aware that I was not free and nevertheless you treated me as one treats a courtesan, as a favourite whom men pass round among themselves.'

(What words, I thought. She's going in strong... Courtesan! Favourite! She really believes we are in the reign of Louis XIV.)

The count gave a 'huh' of despair, but Gulnar, unmoved, continued her speech: 'I don't know what you thought was the nature of my relationship with Otto, but you should be aware that I would never countenance the idea of betraying him. Yes, unfortunately he was already married when we met. He is now in the process of divorcing and as soon as he is free, I will marry him.' (The truth at last, or part of the truth.) 'You cannot imagine, dear monsieur, that on the eve of a definitive union with Otto, I would stoop so low as to deceive him. You would be the first to despise me, and I would be the last to forgive myself.' (All this uttered in a grave tone that was a pleasure to hear. Jérôme lowered his eyes and I imagined he was struggling to keep a straight face. As for the count, he dared protest only with a gesture of his hand.)

'This is the moral aspect of the matter. As for the aspect of reason—do you think, monsieur, that it would be wise for a woman to leave a man who offers her love, respectability, stability, for another whose designs are dubious?'

'Oh,' moaned the count, who moved to speak but was prevented from doing so.

'Pointless, monsieur. What could you say that we don't already know? I would have been no more than one mistress among many for you. Perhaps, I grant you, a little more loved, a little more regarded, but no more than a mistress nonetheless and not a woman one might marry. Very well, dear monsieur: of two loves I prefer to choose the less dazzling but the more devoted. Otto offers me this, and I gratefully accept.' (A little pause here, to make Montforgé feel all the implacability of fate.) 'And there it is: you know what you are dealing with. If you agree to share my views, to understand them, I would be happy. I offer you my friendship, but nothing more, come what may.'

Having finished her speech, she maintained a triumphant silence. I felt then that the count's almost palpable anxiety was filling the room. He was moved, bewildered and doubtless despairing at Gulnar's stern appearance. He was certainly appalled but did not dare show it, for fear of reprisals. Feeling ridiculous, defeated but more in love than ever with this elusive woman, the count got lost in endless 'um, er's. Backed into a corner, he had to declare his joy at having been accepted as a friend, but Montforgé could not bring himself to utter this simple, almost standard formula. Why not? I would have wagered that it was out of a sort of superstition: that his promise to be content with friendship would bind him for ever, would keep him permanently in this dull situation, with no future. I had a flash of insight into what I thought was an essential trait of the count buried beneath his falsely staid exterior: he was a worrier. Yes, he was experiencing a deep attack of anxiety before our eyes: perspiration moistened his forehead, his neck was flushed, his breathing rapid, his 'um, er's less frequent. The emotional sensitivity of a young girl was concealed beneath the cloak of a lansquenet, and I saw all his Crusader ancestors down to the last one abandon him, leave him helpless before this Muslim sorceress.

The sorceress meanwhile was fixing him with a glacial stare, delighting in the disarray she had provoked and which could have gone on for a long time had she not suddenly decided to bring it to an end. 'Very well,' she said with her most affable smile, 'it's agreed: we remain great friends.'

She held out her hand to Montforgé, who grabbed it hungrily and deposited there a kiss that seemed like a religious act. Oh, the poor man must have felt saved! He had not given the vow of chaste friendship but was not being shown the door; he was to be tolerated, he was to be received. So nothing was lost, hope remained, even if in the most unstable form. For the moment he was there, in the presence of the divine Gulnar, the sweet cousin, the good Jérôme. And Montforgé gave in to joy. He smiled whole-heartedly, his large cheeks, his expressive eyes, his nose and even his ears joining in the celebration. It was no longer the sweat of anxiety but the healthy perspiration of contentment that made his face glisten. He was radiant. And to show us that he had given up for good the idea of courting Gulnar and that he felt equal love for all three of us, he invited us on the next four evenings to dinner, the theatre, the Opéra and a small celebration in his folly in Ville d'Avray respectively. I am sure that he would have been happy to offer each of us a large cheque to commemorate this evening, which, despite everything, he believed heralded more subtle bliss. Like every lovesick swain he passed from hope to despair and back again in the face of identical information. My doubts disappeared. I foresaw Gulnar's final triumph, the count's certain defeat. We could expect at most some jolts or shudders, some familial struggles between mother and son, some sudden rebellion of the Crusader ancestors, but the end result was no longer in doubt. This is what I was silently thinking, overcome by the murky sense of envy, admiration and annoyance that we sometimes feel at the success of others.

Gulnar had spoken of the divorce that Otto would be seeking in order to marry her, but neither Jérôme nor I could get the truth out of her: she would remain evasive or tell us to go to hell.

But this problematic divorce brings me back to the one I hoped to obtain for myself, not in order to marry Grandot, which I believed neither of us wanted, but to be legally free.

I had long since stopped replying to the tearful, pleading letters from my husband, who, realizing he was crying in a wilderness without response, had finally stopped writing to me. There was no bond between us other than the, alas weighty, one that a mullah had tied almost against my will one faraway day. Through a psychic alchemy that many of us will know, this event seemed to have happened yesterday and at the same time to belong to a previous life. Imagine a very young girl of fifteen, concealed behind a veil as Islamic tradition required, reading… *War and Peace*, while in the next room a contract was being concluded which would transform the reader into the spouse of a detested man; the girl who dreamt of Prince Andrei Bolkonsky! An arbitrary bond, perhaps, but not short-lived; it was to withstand my rebellion, our separation, a change in nationality. To which powers, which authorities should I apply in order to have it broken? Of course, I eventually turned to Jérôme, to him who knew everything, who knew real life and the other life, the inner one of dreams and imagination; to him who had studied law and who knew half of Paris, with its many teeming worlds. He would help me, I was sure. And since he was kind and helpful, he held various consultations with lawyers, who referred him to a Turkish jurist in Paris, the complexity of my case being beyond their juridical knowledge. These discussions ended in a speech that Jérôme gave me one day in a courtroom style that was not customary for him. 'My dear friend,' he began, which did not bode well:

'My dear friend, you appreciate, or rather you do not appreciate, that the French courts are competent to grant divorce between foreigners only if they possess an abode in France. The rule is infinitely more delicate when one of the spouses lives in another country and the couple do not have the same nationality, which is your case, and is quite rare, actually. Now, having been a Russian subject—I know you would say "colonized by the Russians"—today you do not have a definite nationality, but this is not the most curious aspect of the case. Your husband has become Turkish, but this nationality does not apply to you, as he requested it only for himself. You are no longer a Soviet subject, as you have neglected to regulate your position with the Soviet embassy. You say you are Azerbaijani, on the basis of the paper supplied by the embassy of the same name,' (he brandished said paper, which I had brought him, then placed it on the table to raise his arms to the heavens, a gesture articulating what he thought of this) 'and which proclaims you a subject of this certainly honourable but unknown country. Furthermore, you were married according to Koranic law under the Soviet regime. My dear, sweet friend, do you realize the extreme complexity of your case?'

I was struck dumb, alarmed at the labyrinth that he had laid out before me and which I thought had no exit.

'The French courts are bound to declare themselves incompetent. Since you possess no nationality other than Azerbaijani, which has only the merit of originality, you will have to divorce in the country of your husband, in Turkey. For I should tell you, dear exotic flower, that divorce proceedings require the actual presence of the petitioner on the spot.'

'I don't want to go to Turkey,' the exotic flower cried.

'Rest assured, even if you were in thrall to this unwholesome idea, the Turkish government would prevent you from satisfying it. No government is more hesitant about welcoming stateless persons like you, especially of Russian origin. The government has not forgotten the catastrophic arrival on its territory of hundreds of thousands of refugees fleeing the advance of the communists.'

'Thank goodness for that! But what am I to do?'

Jérôme was silent for a few moments, looking at me with sympathy and compassion. 'We must oblige the French courts to declare themselves competent.'

'And if they refuse?'

'Well, you will get used to it. One becomes accustomed to everything, including an absent husband. No, no, I'm joking,' he added, touched by my look of dismay. 'I will instruct a lawyer friend of mine to start the process, and we'll see what happens.'

*

What happened? A leap into the future tells us that after myriad difficulties the French courts reluctantly declared themselves competent, which led to divorce proceedings by default, so complex that they lasted seven whole years and sparked the interest of the most jaded lawyers and even journalists. At the end of these tribulations, I won my full and complete freedom, which I hurried to compromise by beginning a new marriage, followed in turn a few years later by a new divorce. This is the time to recall perennial new beginnings.

Things Turn Out Well and Not So Well

Life went on: Gulnar grew more beautiful; the count languished; I remained relentlessly mean to Grandot, who to my delight sometimes shed a tear, but he still put up with me. Otto wrote sad, affectionate letters, interweaving the three languages that he knew. An attentive heart could decipher great suffering behind his words, but Gulnar did not have an attentive heart and read these missives without discerning their hidden message.

But one day—the time always comes when the author must write 'but one day'—his letters stopped, and since the last one had been posted in Moscow, Gulnar was alarmed despite her nonchalance. After a long month of silence, an associate of Otto's informed her of her friend's arrest for 'illicit speculation'. He said his case was serious, very serious.

Gulnar shed sincere tears, then quickly dried them to prepare an assault on Montforgé: he had to declare his intentions were honourable, and if not… she did not know exactly what path to take, but things should not drag on indefinitely. Her suitor had naturally returned into her orbit as soon as Otto had left for his faraway business, but Montforgé was hardly euphoric, which was evident to the naked eye, if I may put it that way. No longer entitled to call himself her suitor but only her friend, in the most disinterested sense of the word, he did not dare court her, but his attitude paid suit for him, revealing his turmoil. Finally convinced of Gulnar's honour, he showed her a respect that would have been more appropriate to a dowager than my quietly shameless cousin.

When we were alone, Jérôme called her only 'honourable Gulnar', and honourable Gulnar marvelled at the count's credulity, a striking illustration of the theme 'love = madness'. She claimed he was losing weight and no longer had the fine complexion that indicated a heart and digestive system without a care. It seemed to Jérôme and me that she was exaggerating the count's pallor and weight loss to interpret them to her advantage. But even if Gulnar was overstating it, Montforgé had certainly changed; he seemed to have collapsed into himself somehow. Stuffy and sluggish at the best of times, he sometimes appeared to have slipped into a torpor that was exhausting for him and us. At these moments, Gulnar compared him to a sack of potatoes, but without the advantage of being edible. Torpor, hypochondria, spleen? Whatever its name, this condition was the result of the hard truth slowly dawning on the poor count: he would never be Gulnar's lover. He would never hold her in his arms, other than with a glancing touch when helping her on with her coat or shawl; he would never greedily kiss those mischievous lips that had so cruelly, so inexorably, set the bounds of their relationship. And as ancestral prohibitions rose up like the Great Wall of China between him and the object of his desire, all he could do was disappear, either by killing himself, or prosaically, by renouncing all contact with Gulnar. He did not know about Otto's misadventure in the USSR, for, fearing he would draw conclusions favourable to himself, she would not let us talk to him about it.

I often want to force myself inside the brain of someone who interests me, to spy on them when they are *in extremis*; to insert myself into the slightest movements of their thought, to follow its winding path, grasp its birth, its development, its maturation, its projection outside the cranium. I've never dreamt of the fairy-tale magic hat that makes you invisible and allows you to catch people in private, with all its possible unpleasant or repulsive implications. But to wander through their brain would allow us to understand them, at the level of their consciousness at least.

I would, therefore, have liked to slip into Montforgé's brain, where epic contests might have been under way between him and his prejudices, between his desires and his defences, between the call of Gulnar and the summons of his mother. He must have been so confused at that time, which unbeknown to him was coming to an end! What despair he must have felt, shuffling at the foot of a wall that he could have brought down, had he taken up the hammer of courage, which toolmakers have yet to invent!

For the denouement was approaching, as unlikely as so many events in life that the reader throws in the author's face, accusing them of a lack of principles. You may remember that Jérôme had cautioned Gulnar against the idle dream of millions of young women—meeting a tall, handsome stranger who offers them great love agreeably backed up by a great fortune. Because my cousin was born under an especially large bright star, for her the dream did not appear in a flight of fancy but in the reality of window-shopping one day in the Faubourg Saint-Honoré.

She had stopped in front of the Hermès window. We all, or rather we women, know that beautiful window displays cut us to the quick when they are beyond our means, and would be an affront to social justice if such justice existed. Moving on from this observation, which many may find objectionable and irrelevant to the story, we find Gulnar fascinated by a beige crocodile-skin bag, of an elegance and beauty that encapsulated the achievements of the civilization of the West and of France in particular.

To buy or not to buy, that was the dilemma posed by the handbag. The handbag she was holding, also very beautiful but made of ordinary leather, contained a chequebook that she had only to transfer to the new crocodile-skin bag. The bag was winking invitingly at her. To buy or not to buy? The small fortune that Otto had given her before he left was large enough to last at least two years without having to worry too much about economies, but despite her spendthrift ways, Gulnar hesitated.

Usually, night-time dreams evaporate in the unbearable monotony of the everyday, but this time a dream burst into life, made concrete in the form of a tall young man—the Prince Charming familiar to all young women—who was looking at Gulnar looking at the crocodile-skin bag. Absorbed in coveting the bag, Gulnar eventually noticed out of the corner of her right eye that her profile was attracting attention. She turned her head to see this tall young man inclined towards her, friendliness radiating from his eyes, his smile, his whole being.

'I'm sure you speak English,' the young man said with an American twang.

'I certainly do,' Gulnar replied, in the impeccable accent her tutor had been teaching her for months.

So began the fairy tale. The Count of Montforgé, moping in Saint-Germain, would have to swallow this real-life story. Like a large rough pebble, it wouldn't choke him but would hurt him badly. For Gulnar agreed to dine with John Fitzgerald Kennedy that very evening, to become his mistress the next day, and his fiancée the day after.

The engagement was sealed with a ring from Cartier (the same jeweller that supplied the calamitous Montforgé rose), and was protracted while JFK's secretary sought to obtain from the Administration the documents indispensable to the conclusion of a marriage, a real one that is, not a piece of cheap theatre.

No, of course I'm not talking about the future President Kennedy, who at that time must have been going out for walks with his nanny, but Percy McTadden's resemblance to his illustrious compatriot was to amaze me some forty years later. The same height, the same haircut, the same smile, considered the most charming in the world; and their eyes and mouths were almost identical too. He was so handsome and so optimistic! I made his acquaintance two days after *the* meeting, in the afternoon, when he brought with him the famous ring. It *was* famous too—an enormous diamond as pure as a mountain spring, where a thousand tiny lights sparkled in a splendid firework display.

Percy McTadden was as radiant as Gulnar. Joy at getting the better of 'that wet blanket Montforgé' doubtless contributed to her radiance. He would know what Saladin's descendant was made of—she would plunge an invisible yataghan into the infidel's heart!

McTadden made the suggestion to the inseparable trio—Gulnar, Jérôme and me—that we celebrate the event first at our home, then at a nightclub, preferably Russian. This whole evening, victorious for Gulnar but wretched for me, remains etched in my memory in the finest detail. After dinner we both went to change: Gulnar to put on her only white dress, wholly appropriate to the occasion but minus the orange blossom, and I to put on my flame-red, watered silk dress. I would wear it in defiance of fate, which was treating me so badly. Gulnar would leave me. I would be alone, deprived of her stimulating though also depressing presence—depressing with its constant reminder of the gulf between our fates. But I still preferred to suffer with her than without her.

As I changed my bag I remembered that the postman had brought me a letter from Grandot. The neat handwriting on the grey rectangular envelope spoke clearly of his lack of imagination without any need to consult a graphologist. I hadn't had time to read the letter, which would be no different from the others telling me about his plans for the weekend, asking me to take a particular train or to perform an errand. I was about to open the envelope when Gulnar came to hurry me along, so I slipped it into my velvet bag, red like my dress, resolved to read it at the first opportunity.

The dazzling white of Gulnar's dress highlighted her olive skin, her raven-black satin hair, her generous, vibrant red mouth, mischievous and smiling. She graciously held out her hand to me, her fingers stretched out to show off the sparkling diamond, the seal and crown of a cascade of good fortune.

'Gulnar, you look so pretty!' I said, my heart bursting with envy, jealousy and regret. Why wasn't I her and she me? If God existed, why this arbitrary distribution of fates? What if he was the great mocking tyrant playing with us? I often had these thoughts. I knew there were no answers. I pushed them away as best I could, but they would return, odious and poisonous.

'I'm so happy! It's incredible to be this happy! I like Percy so much more than that stale old aristocrat who I'm going to send packing. And who cares about the title?'

Even with his ten generations of ancestors to back him up, the count did not bear comparison with McTadden, and his strait-laced manners seemed even more ridiculous compared to the casual young American, who oozed freedom and well-being.

I don't think I've ever met a man who gave such an impression of perfect happiness. I don't think he ever appeared anything other than smiling or laughing during the brief period when I saw him every day, his childlike chuckle revealing a lightning flash of luminous white teeth. He certainly had all the elements to be happy: youth, beauty, health, an aptitude for studying and a large fortune at his disposal, that of his father the chemist, who had acquired it by inventing various pharmaceutical products which millions of innocents had taken and continued to take in full confidence. Though later I was to know others, who were equally advantaged yet shunned happiness.

McTadden was also intelligent and well educated. He knew a host of things, loved the arts, had a keen eye for the beauty of an object, and was attentive to others. I'd fallen a little in love with him too, just a little, thank God, but that little was already too much. Alas, who has ever been in command of their heart? It was a love too fleeting to make me suffer, but advanced enough to feel a stir at the sight or sound of this adorable young man who, while wholly in love with Gulnar, thought to be pleasant to me as well.

Just like Otto. Poor Otto—disappeared, swallowed up by a silence that did not bode well. Did Gulnar ever think about him? She didn't talk about him, at any rate, and I was careful not to remind her of him.

McTadden had made such good friends with me that he even spoke of taking me to America, which I refused: we would see later. For the moment it would be enough of a challenge to introduce a single Caucasian to his native Texas. His knowledge of French wasn't too bad, enough to grasp the meaning of the word for challenge, '*gageure*', and he laughed, claiming that no, it wouldn't be a gayjure, not at all; his parents, very understanding indeed, would be delighted to welcome two young Caucasians at once! They had never seen any, and 'oh, it would be so fine'…

The evening of the engagement we arrived late at the chicest nightclub in Paris. We found it packed to the rafters, collapsing beneath champagne bottles, soaked in Gypsy songs, a buzz of every language in the universe reverberating beneath the arches of the cellar, decorated with faux-Byzantine paintings. They found us a table nonetheless.

As in almost all nightclubs, when the music shifted from Russia to America, and especially jazz, everyone started to dance. McTadden and Gulnar rushed onto the dance floor to form the perfect couple—though they didn't know it, it was the sort that Hollywood at the pinnacle of its glory would offer us. They complemented each other so perfectly; he tall and blonde, all smiles and happiness; she so knowingly exotic and Parisienne, as though sculpted in her white dress, that all eyes, envious or admiring, were on them.

We didn't leave the table, Jérôme and I. He no longer asked me to dance, this question having long since been settled once and for all. He didn't dance well, while I found this jigging about in the arms of a man with whom I did not desire intimacy ridiculous, a man who breathed in my face and pressed his body against mine more than necessary. And if there was desire, well really, there were better things we could do.

'What simplistic reasoning,' Jérôme had replied to me once. 'What about the need for rhythm, the joy of corporeal expression, the creativity of gesture that humanity has known since the dawn of time? Don't forget the mystical joy of David dancing before the Ark of the Covenant.'

Mystical joy! Jérôme had the ability to elevate any subject, to which I gave due admiration though sometimes found incongruous.

While we kept our eyes trained on the only couple that interested us, he asked me: 'What's the state of your love affair without a capital L that you are conducting so badly with Grandot? On reflection, I shouldn't have introduced him to you.'

'It's a bit late for regrets,' I said bitterly. 'Our love affair? Limping along. Actually, I received a letter this evening that I should read.'

I took the letter out of my bag. Gripped by the sudden urge to read it, I hoped to find some expressions of love there. I desperately needed them, in my turmoil at seeing the happiness of others. And what happiness it was! The sort that young girls the world over dream of, and not only young girls… I tore open the envelope and took out the letter.

'May I?' I said, mechanically polite.

My dear (the writing was neat, regular, without imagination),
I am perhaps going to cause you great pain, my poor darling,
but it has to be done for both our sakes. We cannot remain
together: the differences in our characters, our education,
our aspirations, are apparent every day. Rest assured that I
have the best memories of the time I spent with you, that I
think of you with great fondness and will never forget you.
Very sadly yours…

His signature followed, still neat, without any crossings out,
horrible, oozing ennui and smelling of the incense with which
Grandot had fumigated me so conscientiously. I sat transfixed,
staring at the grey notepaper. I reread the text that in its paucity
announced our break-up three times. He did not want to see
me again, this is what it really meant; a few lines, a hundred
words, and part of me had been torn away: because yes, at that
moment I loved Grandot; I loved him with his miserliness, his
platitudes, his propensity for tears, his revolting sentimentality.

'What's wrong? Don't you feel well?'

Incapable of speech, I shook my head. I could not mention
the letter without bursting into tears, and to regain my composure I drank the champagne that I hated. Jérôme sensed a drama
but was too delicate to insist, acting as though everything was
splendid here, there and everywhere. I folded the letter, put it
back in the envelope and slipped the envelope into my red velvet
bag. Disgust settled in the bag where the letter now lay, in this
overheated, overcrowded, smoke-filled room, in my soul. I forced
myself to drink another glass before Jérôme's reproving eye, and
since he didn't want to serve me I picked up the heavy bottle
from its ice bucket and poured myself another glass.

Tipsiness only aggravated my gloomy state of mind, giving rise to self-pity, which cut like a razor through a wound; fate seemed so unfair. In one evening it had given Gulnar everything and disinherited me; it had slipped a superb engagement ring onto her finger and this break-up letter to me. I felt I could no longer hold back the tears that rose in my throat and welled in my eyes. Panic-stricken at the thought of weeping in public, I rose and ran into the wings where the cloakrooms would be. An old aristocratic lady, a Russian princess from before the flood, showed me into this peaceful spot, far from the tumult of the revellers, and I rushed into an even more peaceful cubicle, where I fell onto the seat designed for other outpourings than those of grief. I wept a fountain of tears, so abundant, so rapid that my handkerchief was instantly soaked and they ran onto my cheeks and dripped onto my dress, my hands, the white tiles.

They prompted a memory of another tiled floor, on a terrace fragrant with honeysuckle, looking out to the Caspian in the distance: my childhood, which viewed from this closet seemed like the Garden of Eden, free from all suffering. A lost refuge, an abolished world. My tears redoubled, though that had seemed impossible. These untimely memories, I both loved them and hated them, just as I loved and hated Gulnar, Grandot and everything that mattered to me and gave me a stinging sense of defeat. What? To desire so much and receive so little? All my immense pain lay in this phrase.

How young I was. And how hard it was to learn defeat; how hard to open one's arms and close them again on emptiness; how hard to see others reaping a rich harvest from one's desert. Should one renounce the impossible, when only the impossible gave meaning to life?

How long did I remain immobilized in that pit of lamentation, memories and elementary philosophy? Usually attentive to the passage of time, I forgot that my long absence would cause concern. With the champagne playing its part, I was in the grip of some kind of torpor. I saw a correspondence between this cubicle and the suspension of my troubles, as if the tiled walls protected me from new blows of fate. I had to stay there as long as possible—I knew that.

Through the fog of my fantasies I heard hurried steps, and recognized Gulnar's voice as she talked to the noble landlady. Then there was a knock on the door to which I did not respond, suddenly full of acrimony against my cousin. Let her knock, surround herself with a protective air, drape herself in hypocritical solicitude, she who filled her hands with the treasures of the world. I kept silent.

'Open up! You're frightening me.'

Drunk on champagne and resentment, I listened with insidious joy to the redoubled banging on the door and the vibrations in my head, where the alcohol was doing its job. I imagined Gulnar and the old princess anxious and agitated, interrogating, for want of anything better, the white enamelled door on my side of which hung a notice warmly exhorting users to leave the place as clean as they would like to find it themselves. So what if I left my corpse there, drenched in blood? It would be an original wedding gift for Gulnar—but like so many wishes it remained unattainable for lack of appropriate means. I heard Gulnar cry, 'Something must have happened to her! God, what can we do, what can we do?'

The princess replied with pathetic cries of *'bozhe moy!'* ('my God!').

I was triumphant! Let Gulnar know even a tiny speck of the anxiety that flooded my life; she, who was submerged in blessings that Allah, in his infinite injustice, accorded her in profusion.

'We must call a man, strong men, to break down the door!' Gulnar exclaimed.

I pictured the scene: the men forced the door open and it fell onto me, hitting me, hurting me, killing me. And if I was spared, what would I look like, slumped on the seat in my beautiful flame-red dress?

Common sense gained the upper hand over drunken bitterness. I struggled up, pulled back the bolt, opened the door and saw myself through the eyes of the two women who were looking at me with shock. My unpinned hair fell messily over my eyes; my make-up had melted in streaks in the fountain of tears, turning my face into a multi-coloured mask; I was swaying, I must have looked crazy.

'You poor thing, what's wrong?' Gulnar cried, unaware that while she was dancing with McTadden, I had thrown myself into the gloomy consolations of alcohol.

The genuine solicitude in her voice softened my heart, which was seeking affection. All hatred dissipated, I collapsed on Gulnar's shoulder and began to sob.

'Do you remember,' I mumbled through tears and hiccoughs, 'do you remember the terrace with honeysuckle, the Caspian, the devil's house, the rocks in the sand?'

'What's got into you?'

These memories recalled in a nightclub lavatory seemed at the very least out of place to her.

'Don't you think we would have been happier if we had stayed veiled like our grandmothers? We wouldn't have had any problems with work or men or freedom! Children to produce from time to time, outings among women, the hammam... Oh, Gulnar, I'm so unhappy.'

'If Jérôme heard you, he'd say this is sociology for the shop girl, haute couture philosophy.'

She took me by the shoulders, held me straight and studied me—finally, the truth dawned on her face. 'You're drunk.'

I shook my head, and this unwise movement finished me off: nausea rose gently in my throat and I just had time to take the two steps to reach a washbasin. I was told the rest later, and it's of no interest to anyone, not even me.

Epilogue

They married and were happy. But unlike in fairy tales, we cannot confirm the duration of their happiness. We don't want to run and catch the future by its frills and furbelows where perhaps another story is unfolding of no concern to this one.

They married and left for Le Havre to take one of the huge, prestigious passenger liners, which fill us with an unhealthy nostalgia when we see their pictures on advertisements. Western civilization was still a long way from intercontinental aeroplanes that cross the oceans with a flap of their wings, and departures for America retained their sense of adventure—a memory that has been lost.

Montforgé? It goes without saying that he knew via Jérôme of the miraculous encounter before the Hermès window. Footprints from the Caucasus and footprints from America converged at this spot, never to separate again. Henceforth two pairs of feet would walk together in one direction, in one rhythm, with one heart, and perhaps another pair of feet would emerge from their entwinement and carry into posterity that memorable encounter.

We can only speculate about the feelings of Montforgé now he had been 'sent packing', and presume that his pride as much as his heart was wounded by this brief romance. Did he regret his cowardice, the prison of his prejudices? Or was he glad to have stood firm before the enchantments of the eternal temptress? We shall never know.

Otto? We never heard news of him again. He disappeared in the Russian vastness where millions of men and women could vanish without trace, swallowed by the machine of an omnipotent state. We would never know if the accusations made against him were justified or arbitrary. Peace be upon his soul. I was perhaps the only person in the world to remember him for a long time, to think of him with fondness and gratitude. We could not expect as much from Gulnar, who was swimming in a sea of happiness beside which her affair with Otto appeared like a limpid brook, but without importance.

★

I was going to stay alone in the apartment, which was too big for me. I could keep it for a while without material difficulties. Gulnar had left me her small fortune, and McTadden wanted to provide me with a more than comfortable pension. My cousin whom I had so often envied and hated overwhelmed me with largesse.

I was resolved to leave the mentally draining job of a mannequin in order to pursue a more intelligent profession. I was young, life appeared like an infinitely long ribbon disappearing in the distant future. But all these advantages did not manage to improve my mood, stuck at zero on my internal barometer and seemingly frozen for ever.

A troop of us saw Gulnar and McTadden off at the station: the whole family, the Caucasians proud of the 'catch' made by one of their own, and friends led by Jérôme. Everyone was laughing, and I did the same, without feeling the slightest gaiety. When the ceremony was over, I took advantage of the general confusion to flee and returned to Auteuil. It was in solitude that I felt the least unhappy.

I didn't return to the house, but wandered the streets, which still kept their familiar provincial air. I knew them by heart, so to speak: their houses, their gardens, many of their inhabitants. Paris is full of small villages where people pass one another in the street, sometimes for years, where they see children grow up and others grow old, without ever talking or greeting each other. But even these acquaintances by sight make these villages in the city feel intimate.

I was walking through the streets of Auteuil when, suddenly, a young flower-seller held out a bouquet of roses, reminding me of my first solitary walk when a young girl had offered me flowers—perhaps the same one? How close happiness had seemed to me at that time, around the corner of the street perhaps. And if not around the corner, then further on. It would be mine sooner or later. But instead I kept clasped to my heart a bouquet of the flowers of evil called envy, spite, sadness. I turned away from myself, ashamed to wallow in this dark swamp.

I don't know how I found myself in the Bois de Boulogne, coloured by the vivid light of the setting sun. I walked down an isolated avenue, sat on a bench and there, far from other strollers, abandoned myself to despair, sinking into a disgust with everything. The only remedy for disgust with life was death, but I knew I would not take it. How to solve the insoluble?

Searching for an answer, I lifted my head and studied the sky inhabited by a hidden God. A bird hovered just in front of me, and suddenly, miraculously, my heart grew as light as this flight of a bird in the clear sky. Hope was born in the darkness of my heart, fallacious perhaps, but soothing nonetheless. It revealed to me an eternal truth: as long as the flight of a bird, the soughing of leaves, the wash of the sea bring joy to our senses and mind, life remains a precious gift.

At my age everything was still possible, and another thought came to enhance the nascent hope: why not try to write like Aïssé, my Caucasian sister in Paris? Across the centuries, she would guide me fraternally through the jungle of words—perhaps it was her spirit that had inspired this sudden desire?

I rose. I felt so much lighter, not that I was cured of my despair, but I glimpsed a remedy for it, and it wasn't death.

Life was waiting for me. I had to go and meet it despite the burden of my reluctant heart.

'A romantic and gloriously comic account of a heady and
turbulent youth spent on the shores of the Caspian'

Spectator